I0529992

Heartwise

Cultivating Emotional Intelligence for Teens

Teen Edition

Iyla Joshu

A Note from the Author

This book was created using a combination of AI assistance and human editing. I used artificial intelligence as a tool to help shape, draft, and organize the ideas presented here—but every word has been reviewed, reworked, and refined by me to ensure that the voice, message, and meaning align with my values and lived experience.

In the spirit of transparency and integrity—which are core themes of this work—I believe it's important to share this. The result is a collaboration between human insight and modern tools, crafted with care and a clear moral compass.

Because how we make things matters just as much as what we make.

Table of Contents

Introduction

It was the night before her big presentation, and 15-year-old Mia found herself overwhelmed with anxiety. Her mind raced with worst-case scenarios, and she felt like she was drowning in a sea of negative emotions. If only she had a way to navigate these challenging moments with more confidence and clarity...

As someone who is passionate about personal well-being, I've witnessed countless stories like Mia's. Adolescence is a time of incredible growth and change, but it's also filled with emotional challenges that can feel insurmountable. That's why I believe EQ is one of the most powerful tools a teen can develop to truly thrive.

In "Heartwise – Cultivating Emotional Intelligence for Teens," we'll embark on a journey to discover the transformative power of emotional intelligence. Each chapter builds upon the last, guiding you from the foundations of self-awareness to the practical application of EQ in your daily life. You'll find relatable examples, interactive exercises, and cutting-edge research that will help you build an in-depth understanding of your emotions and those of others.

This book's unique blend of actionable strategies and real-world insights sets it apart. We'll dive into the complexities of online interactions, providing you with tools to deal with social media dynamics and maintain a healthy online presence. Through engaging stories and science-based explanations, you'll understand how your brain processes emotions and how you can use this knowledge to your advantage.

As a teen, you face many challenges, from academic stress to peer pressure. Emotional intelligence is the key to thriving during this time. By building your EQ, you'll build resilience, strengthen your relationships, and gain a profound sense of self-understanding.

Throughout the book, you'll find interactive elements designed to help you personalize your learning experience. From worksheets to journal prompts, these tools will encourage you to think about your own emotions and experiences, making the concepts come alive in a way that resonates with you.

By the end of this journey, you'll have gained a toolbox of practical strategies for managing your emotions, communicating effectively, and cultivating empathy. You'll be equipped with the skills to handle even the toughest challenges, from acing that big presentation to navigating complex social situations.

From experience, I know how transformative emotional intelligence can be—and I'm here to help you make it your own. My experiences have taught me that with the right tools and mindset, anyone can transform their emotional landscape and create a life filled with purpose and fulfillment.

So, are you ready to embark on this life-changing journey? To discover the incredible power that lies within you? Then, let's dive in together and unlock the quiet strength that will help you find success in the face of any emotional challenge that comes your way

Chapter 1:
Understanding Yourself

Meet Jordan, a 16-year-old whose day has been a roller coaster of emotions. One moment he's ecstatic about acing his math test, and the next, he's frustrated because his best friend didn't text back. Like many teens, Jordan finds himself caught in a whirlwind of feelings that seem to come out of nowhere. If you've ever felt like emotions are controlling your life, you're not alone. Understanding yourself is the first step to gaining control over these feelings and transforming how you interact with the world. This chapter will guide you through the process of becoming a master of recognizing and understanding your emotions.

1.1 Emotional Clarity: Recognizing What You Feel

Recognizing and labeling emotions accurately is the cornerstone of emotional intelligence. Imagine you're in a heated argument with a sibling. Instead of saying, "I hate you!," what if you could identify that you're actually feeling hurt because they borrowed your favorite shirt without asking? This more in-depth understanding can change how you respond, shifting you from reactive to reflective. Building an emotional vocabulary is your first step. Words like "frustrated," "overwhelmed," or "content" allow you to precisely express what you're feeling. This precision is important because it allows you to address the core of your emotions rather than getting lost in bunch of basic feelings that don't express how you really feel.

Emotions don't just come out of thin air; they have triggers. Maybe a friend's offhand comment lingers in your mind, or the anxiety before a big game keeps you awake at night. By identifying these triggers, you are able to piece together the clues that lead to your emotional responses.

Start by asking yourself simple yet profound questions:

- "What am I feeling right now?"
- "Why did that make me so upset?"

Journaling can be an invaluable tool here. When you write down prompts like:

- "When I feel [emotion], I tend to...,"

you're not just recording your thoughts; you're analyzing them, seeking patterns that reveal your inner workings.

Understanding your emotions can transform your life. Your decision-making improves when you're aware of what you're feeling and why. Instead of reacting in the heat of the moment, you can pause and choose a response that aligns with your values and goals. For example, knowing that anger often leads you to say things you regret, you might opt to take a few deep breaths before responding. There are countless stories of individuals who, by gaining emotional awareness, have shifted their paths from conflict to harmony. One teen used this awareness to work through a rocky friendship, ultimately fostering a deeper connection through open and honest communication.

To strengthen this self-awareness, engaging in practical exercises can be incredibly beneficial. The emotion wheel, for instance, is a fantastic tool that visually represents a range of emotions, helping you pinpoint exactly what you're feeling. Another helpful technique is the daily emotion check-in. Take a moment each day to pause and assess your emotional state. Are you feeling energized or drained? Hopeful or anxious? Over time, these daily reflections become second nature, enhancing your emotional recognition skills and empowering you to deal with life's emotional landscape more easily.

Emotional self-awareness is not just a skill; it's a quiet strength that enables you to steer through life's challenges with confidence and clarity. It allows you to understand your own emotions and those of others, improving relationships and creating more meaningful connections. By understanding emotional awareness you're setting the foundation for a life where emotions are not obstacles to overcome, but allies that guide you toward personal growth and fulfillment..

1.2 The Mood Journal: Track Your Emotional Patterns

Imagine, for a moment, a typical day. It begins with the soft glow of morning light and ends with the quiet of night. In between, there are countless emotions that just come and go, often without warning. Capturing these emotions can seem daunting, like trying to catch the wind. Yet, this is where the magic of a mood journal comes into play. A mood journal acts like a compass, guiding you through the maze of your feelings by recording daily moods and events. Over time, it reveals patterns and triggers that might otherwise remain hidden in the chaos of everyday life. By noting these daily emotions, you create a living map of how different circumstances shape your mood. Was it the unexpected compliment you received that lifted your spirits? Or maybe the looming project deadline that cast a shadow over your day? These insights, when documented, become invaluable tools for understanding your emotional landscape.

To embark on this rewarding practice, begin by choosing either a physical notebook or a digital app. Both have their merits; a tangible journal offers a physical connection, while a digital format provides accessibility and convenience. Once you've made your choice, consider the format that suits you best. Some may prefer a structured approach with designated sections for rating their mood, listing events, and noting reactions. Others might opt for a more free-flowing style that allows for creative expression. Templates can serve as a helpful guide, offering prompts to ensure you capture the essence of each day.

Reflection prompts can deepen your journaling experience, encouraging you to explore the underlying causes of your emotions. Ask yourself:

- "What events led to this mood?"
- "How did I respond to this emotion?"

Questions like these prompt thoughtful exploration, allowing you to peel back the layers of your feelings. By engaging in this practice, you gain clarity on how specific situations affect your emotional state. The simple act of writing can show connections between your environment and your emotions, providing a clearer picture of your emotional triggers.

Through consistent mood tracking, you'll uncover patterns that may surprise you. Maybe you'll notice a recurring cycle of anxiety before exams or a dip in mood during rainy days. Recognizing these patterns empowers you to anticipate and address them proactively, turning potential pitfalls into opportunities for growth. You'll also start understanding the cause-and-effect relationship between your emotions and actions. For instance, you might find that starting your day with a brisk walk sets a positive tone while skipping breakfast leaves you irritable. These insights are not just revelations; they are actionable strategies to enhance your emotional well-being.

Mood Journal Setup Checklist

- Choose your format: physical notebook or digital app.

- Decide on your journaling style: structured or free-flowing.

- Use templates or prompts to guide your entries.

- Think about questions like "What events led to this mood?" and "How did I respond to this emotion?"

This practice fosters self-awareness and builds a foundation for emotional resilience. As you journal, you're not just chronicling your days; you're growing a deeper connection with yourself. Each entry you write becomes a stepping stone to greater emotional intelligence. As you write, you may find moments of unexpected clarity where the jumble of emotions begins to make sense. It's in these moments that you realize the power of mood journaling—not just as a tool for reflection but as a spark for transformation.

1.3 Inside Out: How Emotions Affect Your Body

Picture yourself sitting in class, your mind racing about the upcoming exam. Your heart beats a little faster, your palms grow clammy, and a knot tightens in your stomach. These physical sensations are not just figments of your imagination—they are your body's response to stress and anxiety. Understanding the mind-body connection is crucial because emotions

4

manifest physically, and recognizing these signals can help you manage them effectively. Stress, for instance, might present itself as a headache, muscle tension, or an upset stomach. These symptoms are your body's way of saying it needs attention, much like an engine light warning you that something needs checking. On the other hand, positive emotions, like joy or contentment, can relax your muscles, slow your breath, and bring a gentle smile to your face. Knowing how emotions affect your body can empower you to take control of your physical and mental well-being.

To learn how to tune into these physical manifestations, you can practice body awareness techniques. One such technique is the body scan meditation. This involves lying down or sitting comfortably with your eyes closed and focusing on each part of your body for a few seconds, from your toes to the top of your head. By paying attention to the sensations in each area, you become more attuned to how your body holds tension or relaxation. Another method is practicing tension and relaxation exercises. Begin by tensing a group of muscles, like squeezing your fists tightly, then slowly release the tension. This practice not only helps you recognize where you hold stress but also teaches you how to release it, promoting a sense of calm throughout your body.

The effect of stress on your body goes beyond temporary discomfort. Chronic stress can weaken your immune system, making you more susceptible to illnesses. It can also have long-term health implications, affecting your heart, digestion, and even your sleep patterns. When your body remains in a constant state of stress, it struggles to maintain balance and health. Therefore, learning how to manage stress is not just beneficial; it's vital for your overall well-being. Stress is inevitable, but how you respond to it can make all the difference.

There are helpful strategies to alleviate the physical symptoms of emotional distress. Progressive muscle relaxation is an easy but powerful technique. It involves tensing and then relaxing each muscle group in your body, starting from your feet and working your way up. This method reduces physical tension and calms the mind, creating a sense of peace and relaxation. Deep breathing techniques are another excellent tool for managing stress. By focusing on slow, deep breaths, you activate your body's relaxation response, which can lower your heart rate and reduce stress hormones. Whether you're in the middle of a stressful situation or winding down before bed, these techniques can help you regain control over your physical and emotional state.

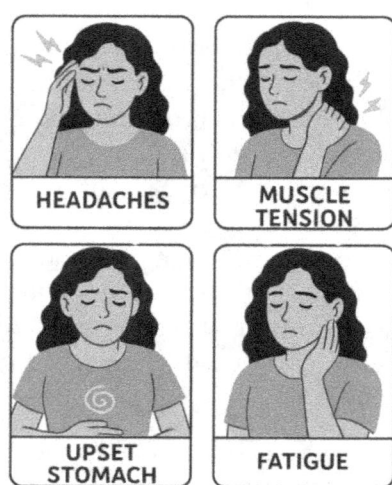

STRESS SYMPTOMS

HEADACHES

MUSCLE TENSION

UPSET STOMACH

FATIGUE

Understanding how emotions affect your body is a fundamental aspect of emotional intelligence. By recognizing the physical signals your body sends, you can take proactive steps to manage your emotional health. This awareness enhances your ability to cope with stress and improves your quality of life, allowing you to experience emotions in a fuller and healthier way. As you build these skills, you'll find that your body becomes a valuable ally in navigating the complexities of your emotional world, helping you to remain balanced and centered even in the face of challenges.

1.4 The Brain-Emotion Connection: Simplified Neuroscience

Imagine feeling your heart race, your palms sweat, and your mind go blank just as you're about to deliver a presentation. These physical and emotional sensations aren't just happening in isolation. They're orchestrated by a complex network inside your brain, a place where emotions and rational thought often collide. At the heart of this network lies the amygdala, a small almond-shaped structure. Consider it the brain's alarm system, always on the lookout for threats, ready to trigger the body's fight-or-flight response. When you feel threatened, the amygdala kicks into high gear, sending signals that prepare your body to either face the challenge or flee from it. This response, while vital for survival, can sometimes be overactive, especially during high-stress situations like school exams or public speaking.

But the amygdala doesn't act alone. It works with the prefrontal cortex, the brain's CEO, responsible for planning, decision-making, and regulation of emotions. Picture the prefrontal cortex as the calm voice of reason that steps in to evaluate whether the perceived threat is real or imagined. It helps you pause, take a deep breath, and consider your options before reacting impulsively. This dynamic duo of the amygdala and prefrontal cortex demonstrates how emotions and rational thought are intertwined, each influencing the other in a delicate dance. Understanding this is important for managing your emotional responses, allowing you to manage life's challenges easier and in a calmer manner.

When a stimulus—a stressful exam or a heated argument with a friend—activates the amygdala, it sends signals through emotional pathways. These signals trigger the release of neurotransmitters like norepinephrine, which heightens alertness and prepares the body for action. The rational pathways, dominated by the prefrontal cortex, then assess the situation, weighing the emotional response against logical reasoning. This process can be likened to a dialogue between emotion and logic, where one may dominate depending on the circumstances. For instance, in moments of intense emotion, the amygdala might drown out the rational voice, leading to hasty decisions. Yet, with practice, you can strengthen the pathways to the prefrontal cortex, enabling more balanced and thoughtful responses.

To make this scientific process relatable, consider the "fight or flight" response during a school setting. Suppose you're about to take a test. Your amygdala senses the pressure and signals your body to prepare for action: your heart rate increases, and adrenaline surges. However, your prefrontal cortex can step in, reminding you of your preparation and calming your nerves. Similarly, during an exam, understanding these pathways helps you keep anxiety in check, transforming a potentially overwhelming experience into a manageable one. By recognizing these internal processes, you can get better at strategies to keep your emotions in check, ensuring they enhance rather than hinder your performance.

The Emotional Response Cycle

- Amygdala activation

- Prefrontal cortex regulation

- Neurotransmitter release

These insights into the brain's role in emotion processing can simplify the science behind your feelings and empower you to take charge of them. By appreciating how your brain functions, you gain a more in-depth understanding of why you react the way you do. This knowledge acts as a guide, helping you build skills to keep your emotions in check, improve decision-making, and strengthen your ability to respond thoughtfully rather than reflexively. It transforms the abstract concept of emotional intelligence into a tangible tool, one that you can wield in everyday life to create more harmonious and fulfilling experiences.

1.5 The Power of Self-Talk: Transform Your Inner Dialogue

When you speak to yourself, what do you hear? This internal dialogue, known as self-talk, can shape your emotions and actions in profound ways. It's the personal conversation that runs through your mind, influencing how you perceive challenges and celebrating victories. Think of it as the narrator of your life story. If your self-talk leans positive, it can uplift you, serving as a source of encouragement and strength. Conversely, negative self-talk can drag you down, making obstacles seem more scary than they truly are. Imagine you're facing a tough exam. A voice inside might say, "I'm going to fail; I always do." This negative narrative chips away at your confidence and self-esteem, creating a cycle of doubt. On the other hand, if that voice says, "I've prepared well, and I can handle this," it builds a foundation of confidence, empowering you to take on challenges with resilience.

The benefits of self-talk extends beyond mere words. It influences how you feel and behave, altering your emotional landscape which helps to create the reality you experience. You can create the reality you want by choosing your self-talk going into a stressful or challenging situation or even when celebrating. By reframing negative thoughts into positive affirmations, you can change your emotional experience. Picture a scenario where you didn't make the team you tried out for. Instead of dwelling on, "I'm not good enough," try shifting your perspective to, "This is an opportunity to grow and improve." Such reframing can transform defeat into motivation. Consider stories of individuals who have surmounted major challenges through positive self-talk. Athletes, facing the pressure of competition, often use affirmations to maintain focus and composure. Students have also turned academic struggles into triumphs by changing the way they speak to themselves, replacing self-doubt with determination.

Cultivating healthier self-talk requires conscious effort and practice. Start by incorporating daily affirmations into your routine. These are positive statements you repeat to yourself, designed to challenge and overcome negativity. For instance, each morning, you might say, "I am capable and confident," setting a positive tone for the day. Another strategy is to actively challenge negative thought patterns. When a negative thought arises, question its validity. Ask yourself, "Is this really true, or am I being too hard on myself?" By examining these thoughts, you weaken their hold on you, making room for a kinder, more supportive inner dialogue.

Self-Talk Journal Prompts

- What negative thoughts do I notice repeating?

- How can I reframe these into positive affirmations?

Self-reflection is a powerful tool in this process. By engaging in exercises designed to increase awareness of your self-talk patterns, you can identify areas for improvement. Use journal prompts to explore your internal dialogue deeply. Questions like those above encourage introspection and growth. Additionally, thought-stopping techniques can help you intercept negative self-talk before it spirals out of control. When a negative thought surfaces, visualize a stop sign and redirect your focus to something positive. This simple yet effective technique interrupts the cycle of negativity, allowing you to regain control over your thoughts.

Your self-talk is a powerful friend on your path to emotional growth. By transforming your inner dialogue, you open yourself up to a world of possibilities where challenges become stepping stones rather than obstacles. As you build a positive internal dialogue, you build a foundation of confidence and self-esteem, empowering you to face life's ups and downs with resilience and grace. So, listen closely to the words echoing in your mind, they hold the power to shape not just how you feel but who you become.

Chapter 2:
Emotional Regulation
Techniques

Imagine you're sitting in class, heart pounding as you prepare to present a project. You feel the weight of your classmates' eyes and the invisible grip of anxiety tightening around you. It's a feeling many teens know too well—sudden, overwhelming, and seemingly uncontrollable. But what if you had a secret weapon to instantly calm your nerves, like the ability to slow time and regain control? This is where the magic of breathwork comes in. Breathing, something so simple and automatic, holds the power to transform your emotional state in mere moments. By mastering the art of breath control, you can soothe your nervous system and reduce anxiety, turning a daunting challenge into just another part of your day.

Breathwork is not just about taking deep breaths. It involves specific techniques that engage something called *diaphragmatic breathing*, where you draw air deeply into your lungs, allowing your diaphragm to do the work rather than your chest. This breathing method is particularly helpful because it promotes relaxation and reduces stress. When you breathe deeply, your body receives more oxygen, which calms your nervous system. The immediate effect is a reduction in anxiety and a sense of tranquility. It's like flipping a switch that tells your body it's okay to relax, even when stress is high. This simple act of focusing on your breath can quiet the chaos in your mind, laying the groundwork for clearer thinking and emotional balance.

To harness the power of breathwork, let's explore a couple of techniques. The 4-7-8 breathing technique is a popular exercise that can be your go-to in stressful moments. Start by inhaling quietly through your nose for a count of four. Hold your breath for a count of seven. Then, exhale completely through your mouth for a count of eight. This rhythmic pattern calms your mind and slows your heart rate, making it a perfect tool for immediate stress relief. Another method that works well is box breathing, which involves inhaling for four counts, holding the breath for four counts, exhaling for four counts, and then pausing for four counts before the next inhale. This technique is favored by athletes and performers who need to maintain composure under pressure, and it can be equally beneficial for you in daily life.

The science behind these breathing exercises is grounded in their ability to activate the parasympathetic nervous system. This part of your nervous system is responsible for calming the body and conserving energy after stress. By engaging in controlled breathing, you reduce cortisol levels, the stress hormone, which contributes to a calmer, more focused state of mind. Understanding the physiological effects of breathwork enriches your appreciation for its power, transforming it from a simple exercise into a strategic tool for emotional regulation.

In practical terms, think of breath work as your emotional first-aid kit, ready to be deployed in various situations. Before a big test or presentation, take a few moments to practice the 4-7-8 technique. It helps to center your thoughts and ease the anxiety that might otherwise cloud your performance. During a heated conflict with a friend or family member, box breathing can provide the pause necessary to collect your thoughts and respond thoughtfully rather than reactively. These techniques empower you to face immediate stressors and build your resilience over time, equipping you with a lifelong skill for emotional balance.

Breathing Exercise Checklist

- **4-7-8 Technique**: Inhale (4), Hold (7), Exhale (8)

- **Box Breathing**: Inhale (4), Hold (4), Exhale (4), Pause (4)

Breathwork reminds you that you possess a natural, powerful tool to deal with life's emotional ups and downs. By integrating these techniques into your routine, you can transform moments of tension into opportunities for calm and clarity. Whether you're in the classroom, at home, or facing unexpected challenges, remember that the power to change how you feel is just a breath away.

2.1 The Mindful Minute: Quick Stress Relievers

Mindfulness is the practice of being nonjudgmental and aware of your thoughts and emotions. Picture yourself rushing through the hallways at school, juggling thoughts of assignments, social plans, and family expectations. In the chaos, it's easy to lose sight of the present moment, letting stress and anxiety accumulate. This is where the concept of micro-mindfulness can work its magic, helping you find pockets of peace amidst the hustle and bustle. Micro-mindfulness involves incorporating brief, intentional moments of awareness into your daily routine. It's about being fully present, even if just for a minute, and allowing that presence to transform mundane tasks into opportunities for tranquility and clarity.

Everyday tasks like brushing your teeth or walking to class can become acts of mindfulness. While brushing, notice the taste of the toothpaste, the sound of the bristles, and the sensation of the brush on your gums. This simple shift in focus can ground you, pulling your mind away from worries and into the present. Mindful listening is another potent exercise. When you're in a conversation, truly listen to the other person, focusing on their words and expressions without planning your response. It's an exercise in patience and presence, promoting deeper connections and reducing mental clutter.

The beauty of these practices lies in their brevity. A one-minute body scan, where you mentally note each part of your body, can quickly center you. Start at your toes and work your way up, acknowledging any sensations without judgment. This exercise is perfect for when you need a quick reset. The cumulative effect of these short practices is profound. Engaging in micro-mindfulness regularly can enhance focus, helping you concentrate better on tasks and reducing impulsivity. Over time, these moments contribute to emotional resilience, equipping you to handle stress with greater ease.

Bringing mindfulness into your busy schedule doesn't require drastic changes. Set reminders on your phone to prompt you to take mindful pauses throughout the day. Pair mindfulness with existing routines, like eating lunch. As you eat, savor each bite, noting the flavors and textures. This intentional practice enhances enjoyment and trains your mind to stay present. These small, consistent practices weave mindfulness into the fabric of your life, offering stability amidst the ever-changing demands of adolescence.

Mindfulness Reminder Tips

- Set phone alarms for daily mindful minutes

- Link mindfulness to tasks like eating or commuting

Embracing the mindful minute transforms the way you experience the world. It's a reminder that you have the power to create calm and focus, no matter how hectic life gets. Each moment of mindfulness is a step toward greater emotional balance and well-being.

2.2 Emotional First Aid Kit: Handling Overwhelming Feelings

Picture a day when emotions hit like a tidal wave—unexpected and overpowering. Maybe it's the sting of a harsh comment from a friend or the pressure of a looming deadline. In these moments, having an emotional first aid kit can be a lifesaver. It's a personalized set of tools designed to help you manage intense emotions before they spiral out of control. Early intervention is key; just as you wouldn't wait for a small cut to become infected before treating it, addressing emotional distress promptly can prevent it from escalating. These quick-access tools are your frontline defense against emotional turmoil, providing relief and clarity when you need it most.

Building your emotional first aid kit starts with identifying what soothes you. Music is a powerful ally in this endeavor. Create playlists filled with your favorite calming songs—those tracks that, when the first notes play, instantly transport you to a place of peace. Whether it's a soft piano melody or the comforting lyrics of a beloved singer, music can shift your mood in profound ways. Alongside your auditory aids, consider physical objects like stress balls or fidget spinners. These items engage your senses and offer a tangible release for pent-up tension, providing a momentary distraction from overwhelming feelings.

Self-compassion is another vital component of your toolkit. When emotions run high, it's easy to fall into the trap of self-criticism, but this only makes the situation more difficult. Instead, practice self-kindness. Writing a letter to yourself can be a powerful act of self-compassion. In this letter, acknowledge your feelings, express understanding, and offer words of encouragement as if you were speaking to a close friend. Similarly, positive self-affirmations serve as a counterbalance to negative self-talk. Phrases like "I am worthy" or "I am doing my best" can become mantras that ground you during turbulent times. These affirmations, repeated regularly, help rewire your brain to default to positivity rather than self-doubt.

Creating a personalized emotional first-aid kit requires introspection and honesty. Start by journaling about your personal triggers. Are there specific situations or interactions that consistently create strong emotional responses? By identifying these, you can prepare strategies and tools tailored to your unique needs. Consider which coping mechanisms have worked well for you in the past. Was it a particular song, a walk in nature, or maybe a phone call with a supportive friend? Incorporate these elements into your kit, knowing they've proven helpful before. This personalization ensures that your emotional first aid kit is not just a collection of generic tools but a carefully curated set of resources that resonate with you.

Emotional First Aid Kit Checklist

- **Calming Music Playlist**: Add your favorite songs that soothe your mind.

- **Stress-Relief Objects**: Include items like stress balls or fidget spinners.

- **Self-Compassion Tools**: Prepare to write self-compassionate letters and affirmations.

- **Journal for Triggers**: Identify situations that trigger strong emotions and coping strategies that work for you.

Your emotional first aid kit is a testament to your resilience and self-awareness. It reminds you that, even in the face of overwhelming emotions, you possess the tools to work through the storm. This kit becomes a trusted companion, offering comfort and support whenever you feel adrift. As you continue to build and refine it, managing intense emotions becomes less daunting, empowering you to face whatever challenges come your way with confidence and poise.

But what happens when emotional overwhelm becomes the norm—when you've spent so long managing stress that you're running on fumes? That's when we step into the deeper territory of emotional bankruptcy.

2.3 Running on Empty: Understanding Emotional Bankruptcy

Sometimes, it's not just that you're having a bad day — it's that you've hit emotional bankruptcy.

Think of your emotions like a bank account. Every time you deal with stress, help someone else, hold in your feelings, or pretend you're fine when you're not... you're spending emotional energy. If you keep withdrawing without putting anything back in — rest, support, boundaries, or time to breathe — eventually, you're broke.

That's emotional bankruptcy: when you feel numb, exhausted, snappy, or like you just don't care anymore. You're not lazy. You're drained.

The fix? You need deposits. That means:

- Saying no

- Resting without guilt

- Asking for help

- Doing stuff that fills you up (even if it's just a walk, music, or saying "no thanks" to drama)

You don't have to hit zero before you recharge. Start noticing when your emotional balance is dipping low — and take care of it like it matters. Because it does.

2.4 Turning the Tide: Shifting from Negative to Positive Emotions

Imagine a time when a setback made you feel like the world was crashing down. Maybe it was a disappointing grade or not making the team you were so eager to join. These moments, often stinging with failure, can seem insurmountable. Yet, what if you could change your perspective, viewing these setbacks not as insurmountable barriers but as stepping stones for growth? This is where cognitive reframing steps in, offering a new lens through which to see challenges. It involves altering how you perceive situations, shifting from a negative view to one that uncovers potential and opportunity. Instead of thinking, "I failed, so I'm not good enough," you might consider, "This gives me a chance to identify areas for improvement." Reframing helps transform what initially feels like defeat into a valuable learning experience, empowering you to approach life's hurdles with resilience and optimism.

To practice reframing, start with thought replacement charts. These tools allow you to identify negative thoughts and consciously replace them with positive ones. Draw a line down the middle of a page. On one side, write down a negative thought. On the opposite side, brainstorm a positive or neutral alternative. For example, "I'll never understand this subject" might become "I'm improving every day with practice." This exercise encourages flexibility in thinking and helps you recognize the patterns that may be holding you back. Another helpful tool is gratitude exercises, especially during tough times. By focusing on what you are grateful for, even when things seem bleak, you can shift your mindset from one of scarcity to one of abundance. Maybe it's the unwavering support of a friend or the comfort of a favorite book. Acknowledging these positives can lighten the weight of negative experiences, fostering a sense of inner strength and hope.

The benefits of cultivating a positive mindset extend beyond just feeling better. Positivity can enhance your mood, making daily tasks seem less daunting and more manageable. This uplift in spirits often translates to increased motivation, driving you to pursue goals with renewed vigor. Moreover, positivity can strengthen social connections. When you approach others with an optimistic outlook, it fosters an environment of encouragement and support, enhancing relationships. Positivity attracts positivity, building a network of mutual trust and goodwill. These connections become invaluable, providing support during both triumphs and tribulations and enriching your emotional and social life.

Consider the stories of teens who have triumphed over adversity by adopting a positive outlook. Take Sara, for instance, who struggled with anxiety about public speaking. Initially, she viewed her nervousness as a flaw, something to be ashamed of. With guidance, she reframed her anxiety as a sign of her passion and dedication. This shift in perspective allowed her to channel her energy into preparation, ultimately transforming her fear into confidence. Or think of historical figures like Thomas Edison, who famously reframed his numerous failed experiments as steps toward success. He saw each failed attempt not as a setback but as valuable feedback, bringing him closer to his goal. Such examples show the life changing power of reframing, illustrating that with the right mindset, adversity can lead to profound personal growth.

Adopting cognitive reframing is like gaining a hidden strength—one that shifts how you interpret and respond to everything around you. It's about choosing to see the glass as half full, even when circumstances suggest otherwise. This skill allows you to reclaim control over your emotional responses, transforming negativity into a source of strength. By practicing reframing regularly, not only do you enhance your ability to cope with life's challenges, but you also build a more positive, resilient outlook. This shift can lead to a more fulfilling and balanced life, where setbacks become the seeds of future success and happiness.

2.5 The Art of Letting Go: Release and Move Forward

Imagine carrying a backpack filled with heavy stones. Each stone represents a past grievance or lingering emotion—anger from a disagreement, regret over missed opportunities, or sadness from a lost friendship. Carrying this emotional baggage weighs you down and prevents you from moving forward freely and living fully in the present. Letting go is akin to removing these stones, lightening your load so you can walk with ease. It's a crucial part of maintaining emotional health, allowing you to create inner peace and focus on what truly matters.

Letting go starts with recognizing that holding onto negative emotions doesn't serve you. One effective technique for emotional release is visualization. Picture the emotions as physical objects, like stones or balloons, and imagine yourself releasing them. Watch as they float away, becoming smaller and less important until they disappear. This mental exercise can create a sense of freedom and relief, as if a weight has been lifted from your shoulders. Another method involves writing letters that express your feelings. Pour your emotions onto the page without holding back. Once written, you might choose to discard the letter, symbolizing the act of letting go. This can be an emotional experience, helping you to process and release emotions that no longer serve you.

Forgiveness plays a critical role in the letting go process. It's not about excusing the actions of others or yourself, but rather about freeing yourself from the grip of negative emotions. Forgiving someone who has wronged you or forgiving yourself for past mistakes can lead to emotional freedom and healing. Guided forgiveness meditations can aid in this journey, helping you to build empathy and compassion. Through forgiveness, you can let go of resentment and anger, replacing them with understanding and peace. Self-forgiveness, in particular, is a powerful tool for healing. It allows you to acknowledge your imperfections and mistakes and to move forward with self-compassion and acceptance.

Exercises that symbolize moving forward can further reinforce the letting go process. Creating a vision board for future goals is one way to shift your focus from past grievances to future possibilities. Gather images and words that represent your aspirations and dreams, and arrange them on a board where you can see them daily. This visual reminder keeps you oriented toward growth and positive change. Incorporating rituals for closure can also be beneficial. Whether it's lighting a candle to symbolize a new beginning or planting a seed to represent growth, these acts can provide a tangible sense of moving forward and embracing the future.

Vision Board Creation Steps

- **Gather Materials**: Find magazines, photos, and words that resonate with your goals.

- **Arrange with Intention**: Place your images and words on the board in a way that inspires you.

- **Display Prominently**: Keep your vision board in a place where you'll see it daily.

These practices of letting go, forgiveness, and focusing on future goals are central to emotional well-being. They empower you to release what no longer serves you and to embrace the present with openness and hope. As you continue to explore emotional regulation techniques, remember that each step you take brings you closer to a more balanced and fulfilling life. With these tools in your toolkit, you'll be better equipped to deal with the emotional complexities of adolescence and beyond, fostering a resilient and empowered self.

As we transition to the next chapter, we'll explore the importance of empathy and understanding, essential skills that strengthen relationships and deepen connections.

Chapter 3:
Building Empathy and Understanding

Picture this: you're in the school cafeteria, surrounded by the chatter of friends and the clatter of trays. Across the room, you notice a classmate sitting alone, staring at their lunch as if it's the most fascinating thing in the world. In that moment, a spark of wonder ignites in you—what are they feeling? What are they thinking? This curiosity is the seed of empathy, the ability to understand and share the feelings of another. Empathy is not just about feeling sorry for someone, which is sympathy; it's about genuinely stepping into their shoes and experiencing the world from their perspective. While sympathy might stop at "I feel bad for you," empathy goes further, saying, "I get it, and I'm here with you.'

The benefits of empathy extend far beyond individual connections. Empathy acts as a glue in relationships, binding people together through understanding and compassion. When you empathize with someone, you're acknowledging their emotional experience and validating it. This validation fosters trust and deepens bonds, creating a safe space where authenticity thrives. Whether it's comforting a friend after a tough day or navigating disagreements with family, empathy can transform interactions, reducing conflicts and enhancing communication. Empathy serves as a bridge in a world where misunderstandings can lead to discord, allowing us to connect with others on a meaningful level.

To build empathy, engaging in exercises that promote perspective-taking is invaluable. Role-playing different scenarios is one such activity. Imagine you're a director orchestrating a play where you and your peers swap roles to experience each other's challenges and victories. For instance, you might act out a scene where you're the new kid at school, navigating the anxiety of unfamiliar faces and uncharted hallways. Through role-playing, you gain insights into experiences and emotions that might be foreign to you, increasing your capacity for empathy. Another helpful exercise involves journaling from another person's perspective. Choose someone in your life and write a diary entry as if you were them. Think about their daily encounters, their joys, and their struggles. This exercise encourages you to set aside your own biases and assumptions, fostering a more in-depth understanding of their world.

Empathy's transformative power is evident in its ability to diffuse tense situations and promote harmony. Consider the case of two friends, Alex and Jamie, who were in a heated argument over a misunderstanding. Instead of letting the conflict fester, they chose to practice empathy. By actively listening to each other's perspectives and acknowledging their feelings, they were able to find common ground and resolve their differences. This salvaged their friendship and strengthened it, proving that empathy can be a catalyst for positive change. In peer relationships, empathy fosters collaboration and teamwork, creating an environment where diverse voices are heard and valued.

Reflecting on empathy experiences can deepen your understanding and growth. Daily empathy reflections are a powerful tool for cultivating this skill. At the end of each day, take a moment to consider a situation where you practiced empathy or could have done so. Think about the emotions involved and the impact your empathy had on the interaction. These reflections reinforce your learning and encourage continuous improvement. Sharing empathy experiences in groups can also be enlightening. In a supportive setting, discuss scenarios where empathy played a role and learn from others' insights and approaches. This communal reflection fosters a sense of belonging and shared purpose, reinforcing the idea that empathy is a collective journey.

Empathy Reflection Journal Prompt

- Think about a situation today where you practiced empathy. What did you learn about the other person's perspective? How did it change the interaction?

Empathy is a skill that enriches your life and the lives of those around you. It reminds us that, at our core, we all seek understanding and connection. By nurturing empathy, you enhance your relationships and contribute to a world where compassion and kindness reign.

3.1 The Empathy Map: Understanding Perspectives

Imagine trying to navigate a city without a map. You might eventually find your way, but not without frustration and wrong turns. An empathy map is a tool that helps you navigate the complex terrain of human emotions and perspectives, providing clarity and direction. It helps you visualize what others think, feel, say, and do, allowing you to create a fuller picture of their experience. By mapping out these dimensions, you identify common ground and recognize the nuances of their journey. This visualization fosters a deeper understanding, making it easier to relate to and connect with others. Empathy maps originated in product development, where they were used to understand customer needs, but their power extends far beyond that. In personal interactions, they can transform how you perceive and interact with the people around you.

Creating an empathy map begins with a simple piece of paper divided into sections: 'What they say,' 'What they do,' 'What they feel,' and 'What they think.' Each section captures a different aspect of the person's experience, offering a window into their world. Start by observing what they say in conversations. Are there recurring words or phrases that hint at their priorities or concerns? Then, consider their actions—what they do and how they behave in various situations. Actions often reveal what words cannot. Next, tune into their feelings. This might require some intuition, as emotions aren't always outwardly expressed. Finally, consider what they might be thinking. This involves stepping into their shoes and considering the beliefs and motivations that drive their behavior. Together, these sections create a comprehensive map that guides your understanding of their perspective.

There are numerous applications of empathy maps in everyday interactions. When conflicts arise with friends, an empathy map can be a powerful tool for resolution. By mapping out your friend's thoughts and feelings, you gain insight into their point of view, which can lessen tensions and help create positive dialogue. This understanding helps shift the focus from blame to collaboration, paving the way for solutions that honor both perspectives. In teamwork settings, empathy maps can enhance collaboration by highlighting the diverse strengths and needs within a group. By appreciating what each member brings to the table, you foster an environment of mutual respect and support, driving the team toward common goals.

Consider a scenario where you and a friend disagree on how to spend your free time. You prefer relaxing at home, while they want to go out. Instead of letting the disagreement grow out of control, use an empathy map to explore their perspective. What might they be feeling or thinking that drives their preference? Maybe they feel the need for social interaction or are stressed and need a change of scenery. Understanding these motivations allows you to address their needs while expressing your own, opening the door to compromise.

Navigating family dynamics can also benefit from empathy mapping. Families are often a mix of personalities and viewpoints, leading to misunderstandings and friction. By creating empathy maps for family members, you get a clearer understanding of their emotional responses and triggers. This practice helps you approach interactions with empathy and patience, reducing conflicts and strengthening familial bonds. Whether it's understanding a parent's concern or a sibling's frustration, empathy maps offer a structured way to connect with loved ones on a deeper level, transforming the household into a more peaceful and supportive space.

Empathy Map Creation Steps

EMPATHY MAP

SAY	DO
"I'm fine"	Looks down, avoids eye contact

FEEL	THINK
Maybe sad or stressed	"No one gets how I feel."

- Divide a sheet of paper into four sections: 'What they say,' 'What they do,' 'What they feel,' and 'What they think.'

- Observe conversations for recurring themes.

- Note their actions and behaviors.

- Intuit emotions and potential thoughts.

- Apply insights to resolve conflicts and improve relationships.

Empathy maps are not just tools; they're bridges that connect us to others, fostering understanding in a world where miscommunication often reigns. By using them, you equip yourself with a powerful resource for empathy.

3.2 Listening Like a Pro: Active Listening Skills

Imagine sitting with a friend who seems upset. They start talking, and while you hear the words, your mind drifts to your own thoughts or the next thing you want to say. This is the difference between hearing and listening. Hearing is passive—sounds hit your ears but don't necessarily engage your mind. Listening, especially active listening, is a conscious effort to truly understand the speaker, not just by their words but also by their emotions and intentions. It involves entirely focusing, understanding, responding, and remembering what was said. This kind of listening builds trust, showing someone their thoughts and feelings are valued. It's the foundation of meaningful relationships, where communication flows openly and honestly.

To practice active listening, start with reflective listening exercises. When someone shares something, reflect back what you heard. This doesn't mean parroting their words but summarizing the essence of their message. For example, if a friend says they're stressed about exams, you might respond, "Wow, that sounds really hard. I totally get it — school stress hits me like that too." This reflection shows that you're listening and gives the speaker a chance to clarify or expand on their thoughts. Paraphrasing and summarizing are key skills here. They involve restating what you heard in your own words, like capturing the main points of a conversation in a brief summary. This helps both parties ensure understanding and keeps the dialogue productive and supportive.

Despite its benefits, active listening faces several barriers. Distractions are the most common. Whether it's a buzzing phone or a wandering mind, these interruptions can derail attentive listening. To overcome this, create a distraction-free environment by silencing notifications or choosing a quiet place to talk. Another challenge is managing internal biases. These are the preconceived notions and judgments we bring into conversations, which can color our understanding. Being aware of these biases and setting them aside is crucial for genuine listening. Come to each conversation with an open mind, ready to accept and consider new perspectives without letting past experiences cloud your judgment.

Practice Exercise: Active Listening Role-Plays

- Pair up with a friend or family member.

- Take turns sharing a story or concern.

- Practice reflecting, paraphrasing, and summarizing the other person's message.

- Discuss the experience and any insights gained.

Active listening is more than a skill; it's a commitment to understanding and connecting with others. Try role-plays to practice. Find a partner and take turns sharing stories or concerns. As you listen, focus on reflecting, paraphrasing, and summarizing the speaker's message. This exercise not only enhances listening skills but also fosters empathy and understanding. Listening for emotions rather than words is another powerful technique. Pay attention to the speaker's tone, body language, and facial expressions. These non-verbal cues often convey more than words alone, revealing the true depth of emotion behind the message.

Practicing active listening transforms how you interact with others. It deepens relationships, fosters empathy, and creates a safe space for open dialogue. By strengthening these skills, you improve your communication and enrich your connections, building a network of trust and understanding.

The Power of Kindness: Random Acts for Social Good

Imagine a small pebble thrown into a tranquil pond. It creates ripples that extend far beyond the point of impact, touching every corner of the water's surface. Kindness works in much the same way. A simple act, like holding the door open for someone or sharing a smile, can create waves of positivity that extend well beyond the initial gesture. In a world where negativity often seems to dominate, these ripples of kindness have the power to enact major social change. Take, for example, a community where neighbors start a tradition of helping each other with yard work. This initiative beautifies the neighborhood and fosters a sense of unity and support, transforming strangers into friends. The benefits of kindness are not one-sided; they enrich the lives of both the giver and the receiver, creating a shared experience of warmth and connection.

Encouraging acts of kindness doesn't require grand gestures or lots of resources. It's about embracing spontaneity and seizing opportunities to make a difference. One simple idea is writing kind notes to classmates. Whether it's an anonymous compliment or a sincere thank you, these notes can brighten someone's day and strengthen bonds. Another impactful way is through volunteering in community service projects. Whether helping at a local food bank or participating in a cleanup drive, these experiences benefit the community and foster a sense of purpose and fulfillment. These acts, however small, contribute to a culture of kindness where empathy and compassion become the norm rather than the exception.

The science behind kindness reveals its profound effects on emotional well-being. When you involve yourself in acts of kindness, your brain releases chemicals like endorphins and oxytocin, often called the 'feel-good' hormones. Endorphins create a sense of happiness and fulfillment, while oxytocin enhances feelings of trust and bonding, reducing stress and anxiety. This biological response improves your mood and strengthens your immune system, proving that kindness is beneficial for both the mind and body. By understanding the science behind kindness, you gain insight into its power to transform lives, making it an essential element of emotional intelligence.

To promote regular acts of kindness, consider setting up kindness challenges. A kindness jar is a fun and interactive way to encourage daily acts of kindness. Fill a jar with simple acts, like "give someone a compliment" or "help a friend with homework." Each day, draw a note and complete the task, creating a routine of kindness that becomes second nature. Another idea is setting weekly kindness goals. At the beginning of each week, decide on a specific kindness goal, like volunteering for an hour or writing a letter of appreciation. These challenges make kindness a priority and provide a sense of accomplishment and joy when completed.

Kindness Challenge Ideas

- Create a kindness jar with daily kindness tasks, such as "write a thank-you note" or "share a snack."

- Set weekly kindness goals, like volunteering or helping someone in need.

Kindness is a powerful tool for change, capable of transforming individual lives and entire communities. By incorporating acts of kindness into your daily activities, you contribute to a more compassionate and connected world. These actions, though seemingly small, have the potential to inspire others, creating a ripple effect that spreads positivity and hope. As you participate with kindness, you become an agent of change, helping to build a society where empathy, understanding, and goodwill thrive.

3.3 Cultural Sensitivity: Embracing Diversity in Interactions

Imagine walking into a room filled with people from all corners of the globe. Each person carries a unique set of traditions, beliefs, and customs.

At first, it might seem like a whirlwind of unfamiliar sounds and sights. However, as you begin to engage, you discover the beauty in these differences. Cultural sensitivity is the key to unlocking this richness. It involves respecting and valuing diverse perspectives and recognizing that every culture brings its own strengths and wisdom. Understanding cultural norms and differences teaches you to navigate this diversity with respect and appreciation, strengthening connections that go beyond artificial barriers.

Engaging in cultural exchange discussions is a powerful way to appreciate this diversity. Picture a group of friends sitting together, sharing stories about their family traditions or favorite cultural celebrations. These conversations broaden your understanding and deepen your empathy. You learn about the significance of a festival you've never heard of or the traditional foods that hold special meaning for someone. Through these exchanges, you begin to see the world through a different lens, enriching your perspective and breaking down stereotypes. Another activity might involve learning about different customs, maybe by attending cultural events or cooking traditional dishes together. These experiences immerse you in the vibrancy of other cultures, allowing you to step outside your comfort zone and embrace the unfamiliar.

Cultural sensitivity plays a pivotal role in enhancing empathetic connections. Understanding someone's cultural background makes you better able to relate to their experiences and emotions. Consider a classroom project where students from various backgrounds collaborate on a presentation. Acknowledging each other's cultural influences creates a more inclusive and dynamic project. This not only fosters teamwork but also highlights the strengths that diversity brings. Stories of successful multicultural collaborations abound, from businesses that thrive by drawing on global perspectives to communities that flourish by celebrating the variety of cultural differences. These examples underscore the power of cultural sensitivity in bridging divides and fostering unity.

Reflective practices are essential for growing your cultural sensitivity. Journaling about cultural learning experiences can be incredibly insightful. After attending a cultural event or engaging in a discussion, take some time to jot down your thoughts. What did you learn that surprised you? How did the experience challenge your preconceptions? This reflection helps solidify your understanding and encourages ongoing growth. Group discussions on cultural perspectives are equally valuable. Gather with peers to share insights and reflect on your experiences. These conversations can reveal commonalities and differences, fostering a deeper appreciation for the diversity around you. They also provide an opportunity to practice listening and empathy, key components of cultural sensitivity.

Cultural Exchange Reflection Prompts

- How did the cultural experience change your perspective?

- What similarities did you discover between different cultures?

- How can you apply this understanding in your interactions?

Cultural sensitivity is not just about acknowledging differences but celebrating them. In an increasingly interconnected world, the ability to engage with diverse cultures is invaluable. By embracing cultural sensitivity, you enrich your interactions and contribute to a more inclusive and harmonious society. Through understanding, empathy, and appreciation, you transform diversity from a source of tension into a wellspring of strength and inspiration. As you continue exploring these themes, remember that every interaction is an opportunity to learn and grow. Each step you take toward cultural sensitivity brings you closer to a world where everyone is valued and respected for who they are.

Chapter 4:
Navigating Social Media and Digital Life

Picture walking through a hall of mirrors at a carnival. Each mirror reflects a different version of you—some funny, some distorted, some almost unrecognizable. Now, imagine these mirrors represent your social media profiles. Like those funhouse reflections, your online presence can sometimes show a version of yourself that's not entirely true. Social media profiles act as mirrors, reflecting not just how you wish to be seen but also what you value and believe. They can amplify your best traits or exaggerate insecurities, creating a digital identity that might not fully align with who you really are.

In the quest to craft the perfect online persona, it's easy to fall into the trap of presenting a false self. The pressure to conform to trends or appear flawless can lead you to post only carefully curated moments, excluding the less glamorous parts of life. This can create a false picture of yourself that's difficult to maintain, ultimately leading to feelings of disconnection and anxiety. To avoid these pitfalls, aligning your online presence with your values is crucial. This means sharing content that resonates with you, shows your true interests, and represents your authentic self. By doing so, you create a digital identity that feels genuine and sustainable and doesn't crumble under the weight of social expectations.

Authenticity online is a powerful antidote to the pressures of social media. It involves sharing genuine experiences and emotions, not just the highlights reel. Whether it's a snapshot of a messy room or a heartfelt post about a bad day, these moments of vulnerability can foster deeper connections with others. Celebrating your individuality and uniqueness online sets you apart and encourages others to do the same. It shifts the narrative from competition to connection, where everyone's unique story is valued. When you stay true to yourself in digital spaces, you create an environment where authenticity thrives and superficial comparisons lose power.

Regular self-reflection ensures that your online identity aligns with your true self. Conduct periodic audits of your social media profiles to evaluate whether the content truly represents who you are and what you stand for. Ask yourself if your posts reflect your values and if they contribute positively to your self-image. Reflective journaling about online interactions can also offer valuable insights. Consider how specific posts make you feel and whether they align with your self-perception. This practice can help you identify patterns and make conscious adjustments to your online presence, ensuring it remains a source of empowerment rather than stress.

The impact of online identity on self-esteem is profound. When your digital self accurately reflects your real-life identity, it can boost your confidence and reinforce a positive self-image. Teens who interact with positive self-reflection online often report feeling more connected to their true selves, using social media as a tool for self-expression rather than self-comparison. However, the opposite can also be true. Constantly comparing yourself to others on social media can lead to negative self-perception and erode self-esteem. The curated images of perfection can make you feel inadequate, as if your real-life experiences don't measure up to the polished lives of others. This cycle of comparison can contribute to anxiety and depression, making it vital to approach social media with a critical eye and a strong sense of self-awareness.

Reflective Journaling

- Think about your most recent social media post.

  - How does it reflect your true self?

  - Does it align with your personal values?

32

- What emotions did posting it evoke in you?

- Think about multiple posts

    - Do you see areas where you are not being your true self?

    - What were you trying to achieve when you posted these things?

    - How can you become more mindful when posting to portray your authentic self?

    - Do you typically post when experiencing a particular emotion?

        - Is this helping you portray your authentic self?

Understanding the role of social media in shaping identity is essential for navigating digital life with confidence and authenticity. By aligning your online presence with your true self, you empower yourself to use social media as a tool for connection and self-expression while safeguarding your self-esteem and emotional well-being.

Cyber-kindness: Building Positive Online Communities

Imagine scrolling through your social media feed and stumbling upon a post that makes your day. It might be a heartfelt message, a funny meme, or a community challenge that invites everyone to share something positive. This is cyber-kindness in action—a proactive way to spreading goodwill and creating supportive online spaces. At its core, cyber-kindness is about using digital platforms to foster positivity, whether through empathetic messages or supportive interactions. It's about making the online world kinder, where everyone feels valued and respected. This approach is vital in combating the negativity that can sometimes overwhelm digital interactions, replacing it with encouragement and inclusivity.

To foster cyber-kindness, consider the power of creating supportive groups and forums. These digital spaces become sanctuaries where people

33

can share their experiences, seek advice, and offer support without fear of judgment. Whether it's a group dedicated to mental health support or a forum for aspiring artists to share their work, these communities thrive on the collective kindness of their members. Sharing uplifting content is another simple yet powerful way to promote positive interactions. Think of how a single encouraging post can ripple through your network, spreading smiles and boosting morale. By sharing what inspires and uplifts you, you contribute to a culture of positivity that can transform someone's day.

The effect of cyber-kindness extends beyond individual interactions, playing a major role in enhancing mental health. Positive online interactions can reduce the prevalence of bullying and harassment, creating a safer environment for everyone. When kindness becomes the norm, there's less room for negativity to take root. Moreover, engaging in cyber-kindness fosters a sense of community and belonging. Knowing you are part of a supportive network can ease feelings of isolation and anxiety, promoting emotional well-being. These digital connections become lifelines, offering comfort and companionship in both good times and bad.

Countless examples of online communities thrive on the principles of cyber-kindness. Consider online support groups where individuals with shared interests or challenges come together to uplift one another. Whether it's a group for teens navigating the ups and downs of high school or a forum for sharing creative projects, these spaces flourish when members prioritize empathy and support. Initiatives like hashtag campaigns also exemplify the power of cyber-kindness. When a hashtag encouraging positivity goes viral, it unites people worldwide in a shared mission to spread kindness. These campaigns often inspire thousands to participate, proving that even small acts of kindness can have a massive impact.

Cyber-kindness Action Plan

- Identify a cause or community you're passionate about.

- Create or join a supportive online group related to this interest.

- Share an uplifting post or message once a week to spread positivity.

34

- What are ways you can think of to promote cyber-kindness?

- How can you put these ideas into action?

Cyber-kindness is not just a concept—it's a movement that invites everyone to contribute to a more compassionate digital world. By embracing kindness online, you can help build communities where everyone feels seen, heard, and supported. It's about recognizing your power to make a difference, one post, comment, and interaction at a time. The beauty of cyber-kindness lies in its simplicity and accessibility; anyone with access to the internet can participate and make a positive impact.

Ghosting and Blocking: Navigating Digital Boundaries

In today's wired world, digital interactions are as vital as face-to-face conversations. Yet, just as in the physical world, these interactions can sometimes become overwhelming or unhealthy. Ghosting and blocking are two digital actions that have become part of modern language, each carrying important relationship implications. Ghosting—suddenly ceasing all communication without explanation—can leave the recipient struggling with confusion and hurt. It often raises questions about self-worth and creates an emotional void as the person left behind tries to understand what happened. On the flip side, blocking serves as a boundary-setting tool. While it can signal the end of a relationship, it can also be a healthy way to protect oneself from toxic interactions. Knowing when and how to use these tools requires understanding digital boundaries and the courage to enforce them.

Setting clear boundaries in online interactions is crucial for maintaining mental health and personal integrity. Digital spaces can quickly become overwhelming with the constant influx of messages, notifications, and social media updates. Without boundaries, it's easy to feel trapped in a cycle of endless connectivity. Establishing personal guidelines for online engagement is key to preventing this overwhelm. Consider what you're comfortable sharing and with whom, as well as how much time you spend online. Recognizing toxic interactions and knowing when to disengage are equally important. If a conversation consistently leaves you feeling drained or anxious, it may be time to step back or even cut ties. This doesn't mean every conflict requires ghosting or blocking, but rather that these tools should be used judiciously to protect your well-being.

When it's time to end a digital interaction, doing so respectfully can make a big difference. Clear communication is a cornerstone of respectful disengagement. Before resorting to ghosting, consider expressing your intentions directly. A simple message explaining your need for space or time away from the conversation can prevent misunderstandings and provide closure for both parties. If blocking becomes necessary, especially when there is harassment or persistent negativity, it's healthy to view it as a step towards self-care rather than a personal failure. Alternative ways to manage unwanted interactions include muting notifications or temporarily stepping away from social media to gain perspective. These strategies allow you to control your digital environment without completely severing connections.

Self-reflection plays a crucial role in defining and maintaining digital boundaries. Journaling about your personal experiences with digital boundaries can offer valuable insights into what works for you. Think about past interactions that felt intrusive or uncomfortable and consider what boundaries could have prevented those feelings. Use these reflections to create a digital boundary action plan outlining specific guidelines for your online behavior and engagement. This plan can serve as a roadmap for navigating future interactions, helping you to identify when and where to draw the line. By assessing your digital limits regularly, you empower yourself to engage online in a way that respects your personal needs and values.

Digital Boundary Reflection Exercise

- Think about a recent digital interaction that felt uncomfortable.

- What boundaries, if any, could have prevented this feeling?

- How will you apply this insight to future interactions?

Understanding and implementing digital boundaries are vital skills in today's interconnected world. By recognizing the power of ghosting and blocking, you can make informed decisions about your online presence. Though sometimes challenging, these actions are tools for maintaining emotional health and ensuring that your digital life aligns with your values and needs.

FOMO No More: Mastering Digital Balance

Picture this: you're at home, scrolling through your phone, and suddenly, you see your friends at a party you didn't know about. A wave of anxiety washes over you. This is FOMO, or Fear of Missing Out, and it's become a common emotional experience in our hyper-connected world. Social media amplifies FOMO by constantly showcasing snapshots of others' lives, often highlighting the most exciting or enjoyable moments. For many teens, this creates a persistent sense of inadequacy or exclusion, as if everyone else lives a more fulfilling or enjoyable life. As much as technology connects us, it also fuels a cycle of comparison and envy, affecting emotional well-being.

Case studies reveal how FOMO affects teens. Take Alex, who spends hours on social media, feeling left out whenever he sees his friends posting about events he wasn't invited to. This constant connectivity heightens feelings of loneliness and anxiety as Alex compares his behind-the-scenes moments to everyone else's highlight reel. The psychological effects of this continuous online exposure are profound, often resulting in decreased self-esteem and increased stress. It's as if the digital world never allows you to truly switch off, constantly reminding you of what you might be missing.

However, there are strategies to overcome FOMO and create a healthier relationship with technology. One method is setting specific times for social media usage. You can prevent endless scrolling and regain control over your time by designating particular periods of the day for checking updates. Engaging in offline activities and hobbies provides a tangible escape, offering fulfillment that doesn't rely on likes or comments. Whether it's joining a sports team, learning an instrument, or simply reading a book, these activities enrich your life in ways that digital interactions can't. They shift the focus from what others are doing to what you can achieve and enjoy in the real world.

Balancing digital and offline life isn't just about avoiding FOMO; it also enhances overall well-being. Reducing screen time improves focus and productivity, as your attention isn't constantly divided between notifications and tasks. You'll find yourself more present in the moment, able to engage fully with whatever you're doing. Personal relationships also benefit, as the absence of digital distractions allows for deeper, more meaningful interactions. In a world where conversations often compete with screens, being fully present is a rare gift that strengthens connections and fosters empathy.

Creating a balanced digital routine involves practical steps that integrate wellness into daily life. Using apps or phone settings to limit screen time can act as a gentle nudge, reminding you to take breaks and engage with the world around you. Consider encouraging family or group digital detox challenges, where everyone commits to unplugging at certain times. This collective effort can make the process more enjoyable and supportive, turning it into a shared experience rather than a solitary struggle. By making digital balance a group initiative, you foster a sense of accountability and camaraderie, reinforcing the idea that it's okay to disconnect sometimes.

These practices help you reclaim control over your digital life, reducing FOMO's grip and enhancing your mental and emotional well-being. The journey towards digital balance is about finding what works for you and creating a lifestyle that integrates technology as a tool rather than letting it dominate your existence. As you navigate this path, remember that the most meaningful moments often happen offline, in spaces where laughter echoes, conversations deepen, and memories are made.

Digital Detox: Reclaiming Your Offline Life

Imagine a day without notifications pinging, screens glowing, or the persistent hum of online chatter. This is the essence of a digital detox—a deliberate pause from the digital world to restore balance and clarity. Taking breaks from devices is more than just a trendy idea; it's a necessary respite for your mind and body. Constant screen exposure can lead to screen fatigue, where your eyes feel strained and tired from the endless scrolling and clicking. It can also disconnect you from the world around you. By stepping away from screens, you give your eyes a chance to rest and your mind the opportunity to engage with the physical world. Reconnecting with nature and the people around you can renew your sense of presence and mindfulness, offering a deeper appreciation for life beyond the digital realm.

Successfully planning a digital detox requires setting clear goals and intentions. Why are you taking this break, and what do you hope to achieve? maybe it's to reduce stress, improve focus, or enjoy some peace. Identifying your reasons helps clarify your purpose, making the detox more meaningful. It's also crucial to recognize triggers for excessive device use. Are there specific apps or notifications that pull you in? By understanding these triggers, you can create strategies to manage them, such as turning off notifications or limiting app usage during detox. These steps lay the groundwork for a successful digital detox, ensuring you can fully embrace the break without unnecessary distractions.

The emotional benefits of disconnecting are profound. Without the constant flood of information and connectivity, you can build increased mindfulness and presence. As your mind quiets, you may find engaging with your thoughts and surroundings easier, fostering a sense of calm and clarity. This newfound mental space often leads to enhanced creativity and problem-solving skills, as your brain can wander and explore without digital constraints. Many people feel more inspired and productive after a digital detox, as if a fog has lifted, revealing a more straightforward path forward.

To maximize your time offline, consider activities that promote connection without screens. Nature walks and outdoor adventures are excellent ways to engage with the world and nurture your well-being. Whether hiking through a forest or strolling through a park, the natural world offers a soothing backdrop for reflection and relaxation. Arts and crafts or journaling sessions provide another avenue for expression and creativity. These hands-on activities encourage exploring new ideas and emotions, grounding you in the present moment. By immersing yourself in these offline pursuits, you create a rich tapestry of experiences that nourish your soul and replenish your spirit.

After completing a digital detox, take time to think about the experience. Journaling about your thoughts and feelings during the detox can reveal valuable insights into your relationship with technology. What did you find challenging, and what surprised you? How did the absence of screens affect your mood and interactions? These reflections can guide you in setting new digital habits that support a healthier balance between online and offline life. You may decide to implement regular tech-free periods or continue certain activities that brought joy during the detox. You create a lifestyle that honors the digital and physical worlds by consciously integrating these learnings into your routine.

As you explore the benefits of a digital detox, consider how these practices might influence your relationship with technology moving forward. Embracing digital balance is about reclaiming control, where technology is a tool rather than a tether. The next chapter will delve into building emotional resilience and shifting mindsets, equipping you with the skills to thrive in both digital and analog spaces.

Chapter 5:
Enhancing Communication Skills

Imagine a scenario where you're sitting with a friend at lunch, excited to share something important. You start talking, but your words tumble out in a jumble. Your friend nods but looks confused, leaving you feeling misunderstood and disconnected. This common experience highlights the importance of expressing emotions clearly. Effective communication is like a bridge, connecting people through shared understanding. When you clearly express your emotions, you pave the way for deeper connections and stronger relationships. Misunderstood emotions often lead to conflicts that could have been easily avoided with clear communication. For instance, feeling ignored by a friend might stem from misinterpreting their silence when they were actually preoccupied Transparency in communication builds trust and allows others to see your true self, reducing the likelihood of conflict and miscommunication.

Expressing emotions clearly doesn't always come naturally. It requires practice and intentionality. One helpful strategy is using "I feel" statements. Instead of saying, "You never listen to me," try, "I feel unheard when I'm talking and there's no response." This shift focuses on your emotions rather than placing blame, opening the door for constructive dialogue. Structuring conversations with a clear beginning, middle, and end can also enhance clarity. Start by stating the main point you want to convey, then elaborate with details and summarize your thoughts. This structure helps organize your thoughts and ensures your message is understood. By adopting these techniques, you strengthen your communication skills and empower others to engage with you meaningfully.

Despite the benefits, many barriers hold back clear expression. Fear of judgment or rejection often silence voices, leading to bottled-up emotions. Overcoming this fear involves building self-confidence and recognizing your feelings are valid and worth sharing. Another challenge is dealing with emotional overload, where intense emotions cloud your ability to articulate thoughts. Pausing to breathe and collect your thoughts can be invaluable in such moments. Practicing mindfulness can help calm the mind, allowing you to express emotions more clearly. Remember, taking a step back and regrouping before continuing a conversation is okay. Addressing these barriers gives you the courage to speak your truth, fostering authentic connections with those around you.

Getting better at clear expression skills requires practice and feedback. Emotion expression journals offer a safe space to explore and articulate your feelings. Set aside time each day to write about your emotions, using "I feel" statements to describe your experiences. Over time, this practice enhances self-awareness and hones your ability to express emotions effectively. Group activities provide opportunities to share and receive feedback on emotional narratives. In a supportive setting, take turns sharing stories and invite constructive feedback from peers. This collaborative exercise builds confidence and offers diverse perspectives on emotional expression. By engaging in these activities, you refine your communication skills and build a more profound understanding of yourself and others.

Emotion Expression Journaling Prompt

- Write about a recent situation that stirred strong emotions. Use "I feel" statements to describe your emotions. Think about how clearly expressing these feelings could have improved the situation.

As you explore these techniques, remember that clear expression is valuable in your communication toolkit. It empowers you to connect with others on a deeper level, fostering understanding and empathy. By clearly speaking your truth, you invite others to do the same, creating a cycle of openness and authenticity in your relationships.

5.1 Conflict Resolution: Turning Disagreements into Dialogue

Imagine a day at school where a group project is due, but not everyone has contributed equally. Frustrations bubble up, and what began as a collaborative effort spirals into a tense standoff. Conflict, while inevitable, doesn't have to be destructive. Transforming disagreements into constructive dialogue is a valuable skill that can turn potentially explosive situations into opportunities for growth and understanding. By approaching conflicts with an open mind and a willingness to find common ground, you not only resolve the immediate issue but also strengthen relationships and build a foundation for future interactions. Consider the case of two classmates who clashed over responsibilities. They discovered each other's strengths and weaknesses through open dialogue, leading to a more balanced workload and a strengthened partnership. This method resolved the conflict and enhanced their ability to collaborate positively in the future.

The techniques for resolving conflicts are as varied as the conflicts themselves, but specific strategies prove consistently effective. Active listening and validation are cornerstones of this process. When you truly listen to someone, you show them their perspective is valued, even if you disagree. This validation opens the door for honest communication and reduces defensiveness. Creating win-win solutions through compromise is another powerful technique. Instead of viewing the conflict as a battle to be won, consider it a puzzle to be solved. You can find outcomes that satisfy all parties involved by identifying shared goals and exploring creative solutions. This mindset fosters cooperation and mutual respect, transforming adversaries into allies.

Empathy plays a crucial role in conflict resolution. By understanding others' perspectives, you ease tensions and pave the way for meaningful dialogue. Techniques for finding common ground are invaluable here. Start by acknowledging the emotions and concerns of others, even if you don't share them. This acknowledgment shows that you respect and are willing to consider their viewpoint. Exercises in perspective-taking can further enhance your ability to empathize. Picture yourself in the other person's position, considering how their background and experiences might shape their perspective. This practice fosters compassion and understanding, allowing you to approach conflicts with an open heart and mind.

Role-play scenarios offer a practical way to practice conflict resolution skills. Imagine a school-based conflict where group members disagree on how to allocate tasks. You can practice active listening, validation, and compromise by role-playing this scenario in a safe environment. Family disputes over shared responsibilities provide another opportunity for practice. Whether it's deciding who does the dishes or who gets control of the TV remote, these everyday conflicts can be resolved through dialogue and understanding. Role-playing allows you to experiment with different methods, learning what works and what doesn't in a controlled setting. This experiential learning builds confidence and prepares you for real-life conflicts, equipping you with the skills to deal with them in ways that work for you.

Conflict Resolution Role-Play Scenarios

Scenario: Group Project Workload Imbalance

- **Scenario:** Two classmates disagree on how to divide tasks for a group project. One feels overwhelmed with the workload, while the other believes they are pulling their weight.
- **Objective:** Practice active listening and compromise to find a solution that satisfies both parties.

Scenario: Friend Group Miscommunication

- **Scenario:** Two friends are upset because one didn't respond to texts about weekend plans. The other feels ignored and left out, while the first says they were overwhelmed and needed space.
- **Objective:** Practice expressing feelings without blaming, and using empathy to understand each other's perspective. Aim to restore trust and clarify expectations around communication.

Scenario: Disagreement During a Sports Game

- **Scenario:** During a basketball game in gym class, one student accuses another of not passing the ball and being selfish. The accused student feels unfairly targeted and says they're just trying to help the team win.

- **Objective:** Practice assertive communication and staying calm under pressure. Work on identifying shared goals and using respectful language to resolve misunderstandings.

Scenario: Social Media Conflict
- **Scenario:** A teen posts a joke online that another peer finds hurtful. The poster says it was meant to be funny and not personal, but the other person feels embarrassed and disrespected.
- **Objective:** Practice taking accountability, apologizing sincerely, and setting boundaries. Explore how to resolve digital conflicts in a mature and respectful way.

Conflict resolution is not about eliminating disagreements but transforming them into opportunities for connection and growth. By approaching conflicts with empathy, open communication, and a willingness to find common ground, you lay the groundwork for stronger relationships and a more harmonious world.

5.2 The Language of Emotions: Words Matter

Picture a moment where you feel a mix of excitement and anxiety, like waiting to find out if you made the team you tried out for or to hear back from a job interview. Instead of simply saying you're "nervous," what if you described your feelings as "bittersweet anticipation"? The power of word choice in emotional expression is immense. Positive language can uplift you, while negative language can weigh you down. Consider moments when you misinterpreted someone's words, thinking they were angry when they were actually just tired. Language shapes our reality, and the words we choose can either clarify or confuse our emotions with others. This is where the distinction between positive and negative language becomes crucial. Positive expressions build bridges, inviting others into your emotional world. In contrast, negative expressions can create barriers, leading to misunderstandings that might not have been intended.

Building a nuanced emotional vocabulary enriches your ability to communicate. Instead of defaulting to generic terms like "happy" or "sad," explore words that capture the complexity of your experiences. Expressing a mix of emotions as "nostalgic happiness" can convey a deeper understanding of your feelings. This richness in language helps you articulate your emotions more accurately. It allows others to relate to and support you better. Encouraging descriptive language fosters a deeper connection with your emotions, helping you work through them more clearly. When you expand your vocabulary, you enhance your emotional intelligence, allowing you to engage with your emotions in a more meaningful way.

The impact of language on relationships is profound. Words can either strengthen bonds or weaken them. Consider friends who, through mindful language, transformed their relationship. By choosing words that validated each other's feelings, they fostered an environment of trust and understanding. Precise language can also clarify misunderstandings, turning potential conflicts into opportunities for growth. A simple shift from saying "You never listen" to "I sometimes feel unheard" can change the entire dynamic of a conversation, turning it into a dialogue rather than a confrontation. The stories of relationships mended through careful word choice highlight the power of language in nurturing and sustaining connections. When you choose your words with intention, you create a space where empathy and understanding can flourish.

To expand your emotional vocabulary, try exercises designed to enhance your language skills. Create an emotion word bank, collecting words that resonate with your experiences. This collection can serve as a reference, helping you precisely articulate your emotions. Writing exercises focusing on descriptive language can also be beneficial. Take a moment to describe a recent emotional experience in detail, using as many expressive words as possible. Think about how these words capture the essence of your emotions. These activities enhance your vocabulary and deepen your self-awareness, empowering you to express your emotions with authenticity and clarity.

Emotion Word Bank Exercise

- Create a list of emotion words that resonate with your experiences. Consider words like "elated," "melancholic," "content," or "frustrated."

- Think about recent experiences and choose words that capture the depth and nuance of your emotions.

46

Words are the vessels through which emotions travel, carrying them from your heart to the world around you. By choosing them wisely, you enhance your ability to communicate and enrich the lives of those you connect with.

5.3 Nonverbal Nuance: Reading Between the Lines

Imagine you're sitting across from a friend who's telling you about their day. Their words say they're "fine," but their slumped shoulders and lack of eye contact tell a different story. This is the power of nonverbal communication, an unspoken language that reveals more than words ever could. Body language, facial expressions, and tone of voice convey emotions that might not be vocalized. Congruence between verbal and nonverbal cues is crucial; when these signals align, the message is clear and trustworthy. But when they don't, confusion arises. Consider a teacher who says they're excited about a project, yet their monotone voice and lackluster expression suggest otherwise. This mismatch can lead to misunderstandings, as the actual emotion remains hidden beneath the surface of the words.

Interpreting nonverbal cues is an art that can transform how you connect with others. Reading facial expressions is key; a smile might mean happiness, but a tight-lipped one could indicate discomfort. Body language, such as crossed arms or tapping feet, can speak volumes about someone's emotional state. Recognizing tone is equally important; a sharp tone can imply anger, even if the words are neutral. Understanding these signals allows you to respond appropriately, fostering empathy and connection. It becomes easier to navigate social interactions when you can perceive the unspoken emotions of those around you, offering support where needed or adjusting your approach when necessary.

Empathy flourishes when you become attuned to nonverbal cues. You deepen your empathetic connections by understanding the subtle messages conveyed through body language and expressions. Mirroring is a powerful exercise that can enhance this skill. You create a sense of rapport and understanding by subtly mimicking another person's posture or gestures. This isn't about copying but rather reflecting their energy and openness. Practicing active observation in social settings can further refine your ability to interpret nonverbal cues. Pay close attention to the interactions happening around you, noting how body language shifts the dynamics of a conversation. This practice sharpens your awareness, allowing you to pick up on the nuances words might miss.

Refining nonverbal communication skills involves practicing activities that challenge and hone your abilities. Silent role-play scenarios can be a fun and insightful way to enhance your understanding. In these exercises, participants convey messages without speaking, relying solely on gestures and expressions. It's a playful yet helpful method to explore the depth of nonverbal communication. Nonverbal communication games, like charades, also offer opportunities to practice these skills in a lighthearted setting. By acting out words or phrases without speaking, you learn to express and interpret emotions purely through physical cues. These activities build your nonverbal communication skills and provide a broader understanding of how emotions are communicated beyond words.

5.4 Role-Play Scenarios: Practice Makes Perfect

Imagine a stage where you can explore different roles, try new approaches, and make mistakes without fear. This is the beauty of role-playing—a dynamic learning tool that brings communication skills to life. In these safe practice environments, you can experiment with different ways of interacting, gaining confidence with each scenario they explore. Experiential learning through role-play offers a hands-on experience, allowing you to engage with real-world challenges in a controlled setting. This method builds competence and fosters self-assurance, as you see firsthand the impact of communication that works. With each role-play session, you're not just practicing; you're preparing for real-life situations, equipping yourself with skills that will serve you well beyond the classroom or home.

You may want to ask an adult to help with some of this; their life experience may help you brainstorm situations to role-play, and they can help lead the feedback discussions if needed. Setting clear objectives for each session is essential to create effective role-playing scenarios. Whether the goal is to navigate a tricky social situation or to practice delivering a speech, having a defined purpose helps you focus your efforts and measure your progress. Encouraging creativity and flexibility in role assignments allows you to step into different shoes and explore various perspectives. This openness fosters a deeper understanding of communication dynamics.

It helps you develop empathy by seeing the world through someone else's eyes. By embracing creativity, role-playing becomes more than a rehearsal—it's an exploration of possibilities where you can test boundaries and discover new ways to express yourself.

Feedback is a crucial component of role-playing, guiding growth and improvement. Constructive feedback offers insights into what worked well and what could be refined, turning each session into a learning opportunity. When providing feedback, focus on specific behaviors and outcomes, offering suggestions for improvement rather than criticism. Think about your experience, consider what you learned, and how you might apply those lessons in the future. Self-reflection deepens the learning process, empowering you to take ownership of your learning and growth. By embracing feedback as a tool for growth, role-play becomes a cycle of continuous improvement, enhancing skills with each iteration.

Sample role-play scenarios can cover a wide range of communication challenges, from navigating peer pressure situations to acing job interviews or public speaking events. Picture a scenario where you must decide whether to follow a friend's risky suggestion or stand firm in your values. This exercise encourages critical thinking and assertiveness, skills that are invaluable in real-life peer interactions. Another scenario might involve preparing for a job interview, where you practice articulating your strengths and responding to challenging questions. Through these scenarios, you build confidence and learn to adapt your communication styles to suit different contexts.

Group role-play sessions add another layer of richness, promoting collaborative learning and shared insights. Organize group discussions where you share your role-play experiences, exploring the strategies and techniques that proved helpful. These conversations offer a platform for exchanging ideas and learning from each other's successes and challenges. By working together, you build a sense of camaraderie and mutual support, reinforcing the idea that communication is a shared endeavor. Through these group activities, you enhance your individual skills and strengthen your ability to collaborate and connect with others.

The exercises in this chapter have equipped you with tools to enhance your communication skills, foster clearer expression, resolve conflict, and understand the nuances of language. In the next chapter we will delve into building resilience and a growth mindset, empowering you to face challenges with confidence and adaptability as we move forward.

Chapter 6:
Building Resilience and a Growth Mindset

Imagine a tree in the midst of a storm. Its branches sway violently, and leaves scatter in the wind, yet its roots remain steadfast, anchored deep in the soil. This tree exemplifies resilience, the ability to withstand adversity and adapt to change. In life, resilience is the inner strength that helps you bounce back from difficulties, like a bad grade or a sudden change of plans. It's not about avoiding challenges but embracing them and finding ways to grow stronger through them. Resilient individuals possess a unique blend of traits—perseverance, flexibility, and optimism. They understand that setbacks are a part of life and view them as opportunities for personal growth. The importance of resilience cannot be overstated, as it plays a crucial role in personal development, equipping you with the tools to work through life's ups and downs confidently.

Consider the everyday scenarios where resilience manifests. Picture the disappointment of receiving a lower grade than expected on a test. Instead of giving in to frustration, a resilient student sees this as a chance to understand their mistakes and improve. They might seek feedback, adjust their study habits, and try again with renewed determination. This proactive method enhances academic performance and builds self-confidence. Or think of a day when plans suddenly change—maybe a long-awaited outing gets canceled. Rather than surrendering to disappointment, a resilient person adapts, finding alternative ways to enjoy the day. This flexibility in the face of unexpected events shows resilience at work, highlighting its role in maintaining emotional balance and well-being.

Resilience isn't a fixed trait; it's a skill you can build through practice and intention. Engaging in problem-solving exercises is a powerful way to build resilience. These exercises encourage you to approach challenges methodically, breaking them down into manageable parts. By identifying potential solutions and weighing their pros and cons, you grow critical thinking skills that strengthen your ability to handle adversity. Stress management techniques also play a vital role. Practices like deep breathing, meditation, or physical activity can help calm the mind and body, maintaining composure in stressful situations. These techniques enhance resilience and improve overall mental health, equipping you with the skills to face life's challenges with a clear and focused mind.

The benefits of resilience extend far beyond immediate challenges. Over time, resilience contributes to long-term success and well-being, fostering self-confidence and independence. As you become more adept at navigating difficulties, your belief in your abilities grows, empowering you to take on new challenges with assurance. This self-confidence is a foundation for personal and professional achievements, encouraging a proactive and goal-oriented mindset. Resilient individuals also show better emotional regulation and coping skills, enabling them to manage their emotions effectively. This emotional intelligence fosters healthier relationships as you learn to communicate openly and empathize with others. Essentially, resilience enriches every aspect of life, providing a framework for growth, adaptation, and fulfillment.

Resilience-Building Exercise

- **Problem-Solving Scenario**: Think of a recent challenge. Break it down into smaller parts and brainstorm potential solutions. Think about the outcomes and what you learned from the experience.

Building resilience is a journey that unfolds over time, shaped by the experiences and lessons learned along the way. As you continue to explore resilience, remember that each challenge is an opportunity to strengthen your inner resolve, guiding you toward a more confident and resilient self.

Embracing Failure: Learning from Setbacks

Imagine standing at the edge of a cliff, peering down into the unknown, hesitant to leap because below lies the realm of failure. Yet, this chasm isn't just an obstacle; it's a bridge to growth and development. Reframing failure as an opportunity rather than a defeat can profoundly change how you approach life's challenges. Consider the story of Michael Jordan, who was once cut from his high school basketball team. Instead of seeing this as the end of his aspirations, he used it as fuel to practice harder, eventually becoming one of the greatest basketball players in history. Or think of J.K. Rowling, who faced multiple rejections before "Harry Potter" became a global sensation. These examples highlight a powerful truth: failure is not the opposite of success but a crucial part of it.

Viewing failure positively requires a mindset shift from seeing it as a personal flaw to understanding it as feedback. Each misstep offers valuable insights and lessons that guide you toward improvement. It's like receiving a map showing which paths to avoid and which to explore further. Encouraging this shift involves embracing the idea that failure provides the feedback needed to refine your approach and strategies. Rather than focusing on the embarrassment of a setback, concentrate on what it teaches you and how it can inform your next steps. Doing so transforms failure from a source of shame into a stepping stone toward your goals.

> *"A bottle of water can be .50 cents at a supermarket. $2 at the gym. $3 at the movies and $6 on a plane. Same water. Only thing that changed its value was the place. So the next time you feel your worth is nothing, maybe you're at the wrong place."*
> *— Author unknown*

This quote can be considered as you are thinking about what you will do differently next time. Do you need to be in the presence of different people to succeed, how can you make that happen? Is there something that can be changed about your surroundings to help you be successful? Do you need different or more support to find success, how can you build a stronger network? What might need to change about where you are at to allow you to find your highest worth?

Strategies for learning from failure can help you harness its potential. Begin with reflection exercises that encourage you to identify the lessons found within each setback. Consider what went wrong, why it happened, and what you can do differently next time. This reflection isn't about dwelling on mistakes but extracting wisdom from them. Once you've identified these lessons, use them to set new, informed goals. This method drives personal growth and ensures that each failure becomes a catalyst for future success. Setting goals based on past experiences creates a cycle of continuous improvement and development.

The emotional impact of failure is undeniable. It can stir feelings of disappointment, frustration, and even self-doubt. However, managing these emotions is crucial for bouncing back stronger. Techniques for handling disappointment include acknowledging your feelings without letting them define you. Allow yourself to feel upset, but set a time limit on how long you'll dwell on these emotions. Then, shift your focus to actionable steps for moving forward. Building resilience against the fear of failure involves growing a mindset that views setbacks as temporary and manageable. By embracing this perspective, you reduce the power of fear and increase your willingness to take risks and pursue your dreams.

Real-life stories of overcoming failure serve as powerful reminders of human potential. Teens, too, have faced setbacks only to rise stronger. Consider Jack Andraka, who, at 15, faced rejection from 199 labs before developing a groundbreaking cancer test. His perseverance illustrates how failure can lead to innovation. Similarly, Elizabeth Blackwell, the first woman to receive a medical degree in the U.S., faced rejection from 29 schools before succeeding. These stories show that failure isn't a dead end but a detour that leads to remarkable achievements. They remind us that setbacks are not permanent states but temporary challenges that, when embraced, can lead to extraordinary accomplishments.

The Growth Mindset Game: Turning Obstacles into Opportunities

Imagine you've been trying to solve a complex puzzle. Each piece seems to fit nowhere, and frustration mounts. Yet, instead of giving up, you shift your approach, trying different angles and methods, believing that persistence will eventually reveal the solution. This scenario embodies a growth mindset, believing that abilities and intelligence can be developed through effort and learning. Unlike a fixed mindset, which views talents as static and unchangeable, a growth mindset embraces challenges as opportunities to grow and improve. It's the difference between thinking, "I'm not good at this, I'm giving up" and asking, "What can I learn from this so I can move forward?" Adopting a growth mindset can transform how you face obstacles, turning them into pathways for development.

Cultivating a growth mindset involves embracing challenges with an open mind. Setting incremental challenges is a powerful technique to encourage skill building. Start by identifying a skill or area you wish to improve, then break it down into smaller, manageable goals. Each small success builds confidence and momentum, creating a sense of progress. For instance, if you're learning to play the guitar, begin with simple chords before advancing to complex songs. Emphasizing effort and process over results is equally crucial. Focus on the journey of learning rather than the destination, valuing perseverance and dedication. This shift in perspective fosters resilience and patience, reinforcing the belief that growth comes from effort.

Feedback plays a vital role in nurturing a growth mindset. Constructive feedback provides insight into areas for improvement, guiding you toward better performance. Seek feedback actively from teachers, peers, or mentors, and view it as a tool for growth rather than criticism. Apply the feedback by setting specific goals and strategies to address identified weaknesses. Practicing self-reflection further enhances learning. Take time to evaluate your progress, considering what worked, what didn't, and why. This introspection fosters self-awareness, allowing you to adjust your approach and continue growing.

Incorporating activities to reinforce growth-oriented thinking is beneficial. Try growth mindset journaling, where you document challenges faced, lessons learned, and successes achieved. Think about moments of difficulty and note how perseverance led to breakthroughs. These entries remind you of your capacity for growth, motivating you to keep pushing forward. Group discussions on overcoming challenges offer another avenue for growth. Share experiences with peers, exchanging insights and strategies.

Such conversations provide diverse perspectives, enriching your understanding and encouraging collective learning.

Growth Mindset Journaling Prompt

- Think about a recent challenge. What did you learn from the experience? How can you apply this lesson to future obstacles?

The growth mindset game is about viewing each obstacle as an opportunity for development. It's about believing in your potential to evolve through effort and learning, transforming setbacks into stepping stones for success.

The Resilience Journal: Documenting Your Journey

Imagine having a personal time capsule, a place where you can document your thoughts, experiences, and growth over time. This is what a resilience journal offers—a space to capture your journey through life's ups and downs, reflecting on each moment and learning from it. Journaling helps track progress and builds resilience by allowing you to process emotions, recognize patterns, and celebrate growth. When you write in a journal, you engage in a dialogue with yourself, exploring the depths of your thoughts and emotions. This practice encourages consistency, inviting you to return regularly to think and document, creating a habit that enhances self-awareness and personal development.

To maintain a resilience journal effectively, consider incorporating daily reflection prompts. These prompts act as gentle nudges, guiding your thoughts and helping you focus on specific areas. Questions like "What challenge did I face today, and how did I handle it?" or "What am I grateful for right now?" can open doors to deeper insights. Additionally, setting and tracking personal goals within your journal can be transformative. Outline your aspirations and break them into actionable steps, noting your progress along the way. This structured method keeps you accountable and provides a tangible record of your achievements and milestones, reinforcing your capacity for growth and resilience.

Journaling can reveal patterns in your experiences, helping you identify personal strengths and areas for improvement. As you review past entries, you might notice recurring themes or challenges, offering clues about your emotional triggers and responses. This awareness allows you to make intentional adjustments, enhancing your ability to navigate similar situations in the future. Furthermore, documenting your achievements, no matter how small, fosters a sense of accomplishment and motivation. Celebrating these milestones reinforces your resilience, affirming that each step forward, even in the face of adversity, is a victory worth acknowledging.

Sample Journal Entry: Reflecting on Overcoming Challenges

"Today was kinda chaotic. We had a group project and everyone was talking over each other—no one could agree on anything. I was stressed out, but I took a breath, listened to what people were actually trying to say, and suggested we just split stuff up based on what we're good at. After that, things started to click. I realized I can actually keep my cool and help pull things together when stuff gets crazy."

The insights gained through resilience journaling are profound. They offer a window into your journey, highlighting moments of growth and transformation. By reflecting on these experiences, you create a deeper understanding of yourself, your values, and your aspirations. This practice nurtures self-compassion, reminding you that progress is a continuous process, not a destination. It allows you to embrace your imperfections, seeing them as opportunities for learning and growth rather than obstacles. As you continue to document your journey, you'll find that each entry, each reflection, is a building block, laying the foundation for a resilient and empowered self.

Real-Life Resilience: Stories from Inspiring Teens

Consider the story of Ana, a high school sophomore whose world turned upside down when her family faced financial difficulties, forcing them to move to a new city. Losing her friends and familiar surroundings, Ana initially felt lost and overwhelmed. Yet, she slowly began to carve out a place for herself in this new environment. She joined the school's debate team, channeling her emotions into refining her skills. Despite the initial fear and loneliness, Ana's determination paid off as she won several competitions, gaining confidence and a sense of belonging. Her story is a testament to the power of resilience, showing that despite adversity, strength and perseverance can lead to unexpected and rewarding paths.

Then there's Jamal, who faced bullying during his middle school years because he was different—quiet, artistic, and more interested in drawing comics than playing sports. Instead of letting this treatment define him, Jamal found solace in art. He began drawing comics about a superhero who, much like himself, felt out of place but learned to embrace his unique talents. These comics became popular among his peers, making Jamal a school celebrity. His resilience transformed his pain into creativity, illustrating how hardships can be catalysts for personal growth and community connection. Jamal's journey highlights the importance of staying true to oneself and finding strength in vulnerability.

From these stories, several key lessons emerge. Perseverance and determination are central to overcoming adversity. Ana and Jamal both faced major challenges, yet they pushed through, using their experiences as stepping stones rather than stumbling blocks. Their stories underscore that setbacks aren't the end of the road but rather opportunities for reinvention and growth. Another crucial element in their journeys was the presence of support systems. Whether it was a mentor on the debate team for Ana or a teacher who encouraged Jamal's artistic talents, having someone to believe in you can make all the difference. It reminds us that resilience is not built in isolation; it thrives on connections and community.

Reflecting on these stories invites you to consider your own life. What challenges have you faced, and how did you respond? Are there moments where you, like Ana and Jamal, found unexpected strength? Identifying the strategies that helped you can be empowering. Maybe it was seeking help, finding an outlet, or simply refusing to give up. These strategies can become part of your personal resilience toolkit, ready to be called upon when needed. Setting goals based on the inspiration drawn from others can also be a powerful motivator. By envisioning where you want to go, you create a roadmap for your resilience journey, guided by the successes of those who have walked similar paths.

Connecting with resilient peers can deepen your understanding and application of these concepts. Participating in peer-led resilience workshops or storytelling sessions provides a platform for sharing experiences and learning from others. These interactions foster a sense of camaraderie as you realize you're not alone in facing life's challenges. Group projects focused on resilience-building activities also offer opportunities to collaborate and grow together. Working collectively gives you insights into different resilience strategies and perspectives, enriching your approach.

This chapter has explored the power of real-life stories and the lessons they impart, showcasing resilience's role in overcoming adversity. As you think about these stories and your own experiences, remember that resilience is a journey of growth and transformation. It's about finding strength in challenges, drawing inspiration from others, and forging connections that support your personal growth. In the next chapter, we'll delve into how emotional intelligence can be seamlessly integrated into your daily life, enhancing your relationships and personal growth.

Chapter 7
Real-World Scenarios

Imagine standing in the center of a bustling school hallway, surrounded by a whirlwind of chatter, lockers slamming, and students rushing to their next class. This chaos is a familiar backdrop for many teens as they deal with the pressures of academic life. For many, school isn't just a place of learning; it's a battleground of stressors that can feel overwhelming. From the pressure of securing top grades to the looming deadlines of assignments, the weight of these challenges can take a toll on both emotional and mental health. Understanding and managing this stress is crucial, not only for academic success but also for overall well-being.

One of the primary sources of stress in school is the pressure from exams and grades. The expectation to perform well can weigh heavily on students, creating anxiety that affects both sleep and concentration. It's not just the exams themselves; the anticipation and fear of not meeting expectations can be paralyzing. Time management adds another layer of complexity. Balancing multiple assignments with personal commitments can often feel like juggling flaming torches. The constant race against deadlines can lead to burnout, affecting mood and academic performance. Recognizing these stressors is the first step in addressing them.

To combat academic stress, it's essential to create strategies that promote balance and well-being. Creating a study schedule is a practical way to manage your workload. By breaking tasks into smaller, manageable parts and allocating specific times for each, you make a roadmap that reduces last-minute cramming and provides a sense of control. Complementing this with relaxation techniques can further ease the burden. Before exams, consider practicing deep breathing exercises or progressive muscle relaxation. These methods can calm nerves, enhance focus, and improve performance by reducing stress responses in the body. They offer a moment of relief amid chaos, allowing you to approach challenges with a clearer mind.

Adopting a positive mindset plays a pivotal role in managing academic stress. Shifting focus from grades to the learning process itself can alleviate the pressure to achieve perfection. Emphasizing effort and growth over results fosters a healthier relationship with learning. Setting realistic and achievable goals is equally important. By defining clear, attainable objectives, you can celebrate small victories, boosting motivation and confidence. This method lessens stress and builds resilience, preparing you to tackle future challenges with an optimistic outlook.

Consider the story of Emma, a high school student who struggled with pre-exam anxiety. Initially overwhelmed, she decided to incorporate mindfulness techniques into her routine. She learned to calm her mind and reduce her stress by practicing meditation and focusing on her breath. This not only improved her academic performance but also her overall well-being. Another example is a group of friends who formed a study group to support one another. By sharing resources and encouraging each other, they enhanced their understanding of the material and built a supportive community that eased individual pressures.

Stress Management Reflection Exercise

Think about a recent school challenge. Identify the primary stressors and consider which strategies from this chapter might help you manage these pressures. Write a short plan detailing how you will implement these techniques in your daily routine.

These strategies and stories underscore the importance of addressing academic stress with proactive measures. By creating effective habits and fostering a positive mindset, you can transform the school environment from a source of stress into a place of growth and opportunity.

7.1 Friendship Drama: Navigating Social Circles

Navigating the intricate web of teenage friendships can feel like walking on a tightrope. One minute, everything is harmonious, and the next, you find yourself tangled in a web of misunderstandings and rumors. These are common sources of drama in social circles, often stemming from miscommunication or a casual remark that spirals out of control. There's the instance when a friend might misinterpret a text message, leading to confusion and, potentially, a rift. Or when a joke, meant to be lighthearted, is taken the wrong way, causing feelings to be hurt. Rumors, too, can spread like wildfire, fueled by snippets of truth mixed with exaggeration, turning minor issues into major conflicts.

Jealousy and competition are other culprits that can disrupt friendships. It's natural to feel envious when a friend excels in an area where you struggle, whether it's academics, sports, or social popularity. However, when left unchecked, jealousy can breed resentment and create distance. This is especially true when friends compare themselves to one another, feeling that they must outdo each other to maintain their self-worth. The resulting competition can erode the foundation of trust and support that genuine friendships are built upon.

Open and honest communication is key to resolving these conflicts constructively. It's crucial to talk directly with the individuals involved and address issues head-on rather than letting them fester. When engaging in these conversations, it's important to express your feelings clearly and listen actively, validating the emotions of others. This method fosters understanding and helps to clear up misunderstandings. Establishing clear boundaries is another helpful strategy. By setting limits on what is acceptable behavior within the friendship, you create mutual respect that can prevent future conflicts.

Empathy plays a vital role in strengthening friendships and preventing drama. It involves stepping into your friend's shoes and seeing the world from their perspective. This understanding can transform how you respond to conflicts, shifting the focus from blame to resolution. When friends share their struggles, listening without judgment and acknowledging their feelings is essential, even if you disagree with their viewpoint. By doing so, you show that you care about their experience, which can strengthen the bond between you both.

Consider the story of a group of friends who found themselves entangled in a rumor that threatened to tear them apart. Initially, emotions ran high, but they decided to address the issue collectively. Sitting down and discussing what happened, they realized the rumor was based on a misunderstanding. Through open dialogue and a willingness to listen, they were able to clear the air and restore trust. Another example involves a teenager who felt overshadowed by her best friend's achievements. Instead of letting jealousy take root, she chose to communicate her feelings honestly. This led to a heartfelt conversation where they discussed their insecurities and reaffirmed their support for each other.

Conflict Resolution Checklist

- Identify the core issue causing conflict.

- Come to the conversation with a calm and open mindset.

- Use "I feel" statements to express emotions without blame.

- Listen actively and validate the other person's feelings.

- Set clear boundaries and discuss ways to prevent future conflicts.

These scenarios highlight how friendship drama can be transformed into opportunities for growth and a more profound connection with the right tools and mindset. By valuing empathy and open communication, you can confidently navigate the ups and downs of social circles.

7.2 Family Dynamics: Understanding and Communicating at Home

Imagine a bustling kitchen filled with the aroma of dinner, where conversations weave through the air like a tapestry. Yet, beneath this lively scene, a silent tension may simmer. Family dynamics often present unique challenges, with communication styles being one of the biggest hurdles. Generational differences can create misunderstandings; parents might value direct conversations, while teens may prefer more casual, indirect exchanges. These differences can lead to conflicts over responsibilities and expectations, where what seems reasonable to one generation feels overwhelming to another. For example, parents might expect teens to manage chores and schoolwork effortlessly, not realizing the stress it adds to their already packed schedules.

To bridge these gaps, fostering positive family communication can make a world of difference. Establishing regular family meetings can be a game-changer. These gatherings create a dedicated space for everyone to voice concerns and share updates, fostering a sense of inclusion and cooperation. During these meetings, encouraging the use of "I feel" statements helps family members express emotions without casting blame. Instead of saying, "You never help with the dishes," one might say, "I feel overwhelmed when I have to manage all the chores alone." This simple shift in language can diffuse tension and open the door for constructive dialogue, allowing family members to express themselves honestly while minimizing defensive reactions.

Empathy plays a crucial role in strengthening family bonds. Understanding parents' perspectives helps teens appreciate the pressures adults face, such as work stress or financial concerns. In turn, parents who practice patience and active listening with their children can better comprehend the challenges teens encounter, from social pressures to academic demands. This mutual understanding fosters an environment where individuals feel heard and valued, reducing the likelihood of misunderstandings and conflicts. Siblings, too, benefit from empathy by learning to recognize each other's strengths and appreciating their unique contributions to the family dynamic.

Consider a family that often found themselves arguing over weekend plans. The parents wanted structured family activities, while the teens preferred spontaneous outings with friends. They decided to hold a family meeting to discuss the recurring issue. By using "I feel" statements and actively listening to each other, they discovered that the parents valued quality time together. At the same time, the teens needed personal freedom to explore their interests. Through empathy and compromise, they created a schedule that balanced family activities with individual pursuits, transforming potential conflict into a harmonious agreement. Another example involved two siblings who frequently clashed over shared responsibilities, like cleaning their shared room. By acknowledging each other's strengths and discussing their preferences, they created a system that divided tasks according to what each enjoyed, fostering cooperation and reducing friction.

These scenarios highlight the transformative power of empathy and communication in resolving family tensions. Families can build stronger, more empathetic relationships by recognizing and appreciating each other's perspectives. This method addresses immediate issues and lays the foundation for healthier, more supportive interactions in the future. Through regular communication and a commitment to understanding, family members can work through the complexities of home life with greater ease and mutual respect.

7.3 Sportsmanship: Emotions on the Field

Imagine standing on a sunlit field. the referee blowing his whistle, signaling the start of a game. The adrenaline rushes through you as the competition heats up. Sports are more than just physical contests; they're an onslaught of emotions that test your courage and your ability to work within a team. The pressure of competition can be intense, with every player striving to outperform the other. Winning brings elation, while losing can sting like a fresh wound. These emotional highs and lows are part of the athletic journey, each game a small-scale version of life's broader challenges. Managing these emotions is key to not just surviving but thriving in sports.

To deal with the emotional landscape of sports, athletes need strategies to maintain composure and focus. Visualization exercises can be particularly helpful. Picture yourself scoring a goal or executing a perfect play. This mental rehearsal prepares your mind for success, boosting confidence and reducing anxiety. It's like seeing a map before embarking on a journey; you know the terrain and can confidently navigate it. Before a match, breathing techniques such as deep breathing can help calm nerves. Slow, deliberate breaths can slow your heart rate and center your thoughts, allowing you to channel your energy into the game. These techniques enable you to control your physiological responses and focus clearly, even under pressure.

Beyond individual performance, sportsmanship emphasizes respect and fairness. It's about playing with integrity, encouraging teammates, and respecting opponents. A true athlete understands that the spirit of the game transcends personal achievement. Encouraging teammates during a match can lift morale and foster a sense of unity. Whether it's a pat on the back or a simple "You've got this," such gestures can transform the team's dynamics, bolstering everyone's confidence. Accepting defeat is equally important. Learning to lose with dignity and viewing it as an opportunity for growth is a hallmark of good sportsmanship. It's about acknowledging the effort of others and finding lessons in every setback.

Consider the story of a soccer team that rallied around a member who missed a crucial penalty shot. Instead of blame, they offered support, reminding him that everyone makes mistakes. This act of solidarity strengthened their bond and inspired him to perform better in future games. After a challenging tennis match, another athlete congratulated her opponent with sincerity. Despite her loss, she recognized the dedication it took for her competitor to win. These examples of emotional intelligence on the field highlight how sportsmanship can elevate the game experience, turning competition into friendship.

Sports teach us about more than just physical competency; they offer lessons in emotional resilience and teamwork. By mastering the emotional aspects of athletics, you gain skills that extend beyond the field. Whether it's staying calm under pressure, supporting others, or learning from losses, these lessons prepare you for life's broader challenges. Each game becomes a rehearsal for real-world encounters, shaping you into a more balanced and empathetic individual.

7.4 Facing Rejection: Constructive Coping Strategies

Rejection. Just the word itself can sting, bringing with it a flood of emotions that can feel overwhelming. Whether it's not making the cut for a sports team, being turned down for a date, or receiving a college rejection letter, these experiences can profoundly impact self-esteem. In social settings, rejection might make you question your worth or where you fit in, leading to feelings of isolation. Academically, it might feel like a personal failure, casting a shadow over your achievements and efforts. The internal dialogue that follows rejection can be harsh, echoing with thoughts of inadequacy and self-doubt. These common experiences can chip away at your self-worth if left unchecked, making it crucial to address the emotional aftermath head-on.

Reframing rejection as a learning opportunity is a powerful way to shift your perspective. Instead of viewing it as a definitive judgment of your abilities or character, consider it as feedback that guides your growth. This doesn't mean dismissing the disappointment or hurt but rather using it to fuel your determination. Seek feedback wherever possible. Understanding why you didn't achieve your goal can provide valuable insights and help you set new, realistic targets. For instance, if a college application falls short, analyzing areas for improvement can prepare you for future success. Setting new goals based on this feedback turns rejection into a stepping stone rather than a stumbling block, encouraging resilience and perseverance.

Practicing self-compassion is essential in coping with rejection. It's about being gentle with yourself and recognizing that setbacks are a part of life, not a reflection of your worth. Affirmations can play an important role in bolstering self-esteem. Simple phrases like "I am capable" or "I am worthy" repeated regularly can counteract negative self-talk and reinforce a positive self-image. Alongside affirmations, engaging in self-care activities can restore emotional balance. Whether it's taking a long walk, diving into a good book, or spending time with friends, nurturing yourself helps heal the wounds of rejection and renews your sense of well-being.

Consider the story of a student who faced college rejection. Initially devastated, she chose to view the experience as a chance to better her application. By seeking feedback from mentors and focusing on strengthening her skills, she improved her future applications and discovered a renewed passion for learning. Similarly, think of a teen who felt excluded from a social group. Instead of letting this define him, he ventured into new activities, meeting people who shared his interests and values. This expanded his social circle and boosted his confidence, showing that rejection can lead to unexpected and rewarding paths.

Rejection is an inevitable part of life, but it doesn't have to define you. You can deal with the emotional waves it brings and emerge stronger by approaching it with a growth mindset and self-compassion. These experiences teach resilience, highlighting the importance of perseverance and adaptability in personal and academic pursuits. As you think about these strategies, remember that every setback carries the potential for growth, shaping you into a more resilient and self-assured individual. With each rejection faced and overcome, you build a foundation of strength that prepares you for future challenges, equipping you with the tools to thrive in an ever-changing world.

Chapter 8:
Mindfulness and Well-Being Practices

Imagine waking up to the gentle brush of morning light seeping through your window, the world still quiet, like a blank canvas waiting for your brushstrokes. This serene moment is the perfect opportunity to set the tone for the rest of your day. Mindful mornings are not just a trendy concept; they are a powerful practice that can transform the chaos of everyday life into a symphony of calm and clarity. Starting your day with mindfulness can provide a foundation of peace and focus, allowing you to manage challenges with grace and resilience. For teens and their parents alike, incorporating mindfulness into the morning routine can be a game-changer, offering benefits that ripple through the day.

The intention to begin the day with purpose and presence is at the heart of mindful mornings. It's about creating a routine, prioritizing mental and emotional well-being rather than rushing into the day with a bunch of distractions. The benefits of a mindful morning are multifaceted. By beginning your day with clarity and calm, you set the stage for increased focus and concentration during daily activities. This heightened awareness enhances productivity and builds emotional resilience, equipping you to handle stress and setbacks with a balanced mindset. Practicing mindfulness in the morning serves as a mental reset, clearing the fog of sleep and bringing a fresh perspective to the tasks ahead.

Creating a morning routine that includes mindfulness doesn't require drastic changes to your schedule. It can be as simple as dedicating a few minutes to meditation or setting intentions for the day through positive affirmations. Morning meditation sessions provide a quiet space to center your thoughts and connect with yourself before the day's demands take over. Find a comfortable spot, close your eyes, and focus on your breath, letting thoughts come and go like passing clouds. This brief interlude of stillness can ground you, fostering a sense of peace and readiness to face whatever comes your way. Similarly, setting intentions for the day through affirmations can be a powerful practice. Affirmations are positive statements that reflect your goals and values. Repeating them each morning aligns your mindset with your aspirations, infusing your day with purpose and positivity.

The benefits of mindful mornings extends beyond just the morning hours. By starting your day with mindfulness, you encourage a mindset that carries through your daily activities. Increased focus and concentration are natural byproducts of a clear and calm mind. You're better equipped to tackle tasks efficiently, keeping distractions at bay. Moreover, the emotional resilience built through morning mindfulness empowers you to deal with the ups and downs of the day with steadiness and grace. Stressful situations become opportunities to practice patience and composure rather than triggers for anxiety or frustration. This resilience is not just beneficial for you but also creates a ripple effect, positively influencing your interactions with others.

Below is an example of a 10-minute guided meditation before breakfast. This simple practice lets you ease into the day, clearing mental clutter and setting a peaceful tone. By focusing on your breath and gently releasing tension, you relax into a sense of renewal, ready to embrace the day ahead. Another practice to incorporate could be stretching exercises combined with mindful breathing. As you stretch, focus on each movement and breath, feeling the sensations in your body. This prepares your body physically and centers your mind, enhancing your awareness and presence.

Create Your Morning Mindfulness Routine

- **Choose a Quiet Space**: Find a peaceful spot where you won't be disturbed.

- **Set a Timer**: Dedicate at least 5-10 minutes to your practice.

- **Select a Mindful Activity**: Whether meditation, stretching, or affirmations, choose what resonates with you.

- **Reflect**: After your practice, take a moment to notice how you feel and any changes in your mindset.

Integrating mindful practices into your morning routine lays the groundwork for a fulfilling and balanced day. The clarity and calm achieved in those first moments can shape your day, turning routine activities into mindful experiences.

8.1 The Body Scan: Tuning into Physical and Emotional Sensations

Imagine lying flat on your back, eyes gently closed, as you embark on an inner exploration. The body scan is a mindfulness practice that invites you to tune into the physical sensations within your body. It's a simple yet profound way to enhance your connection between mind and body by recognizing areas of tension and relaxation. This awareness is crucial because it helps you understand how emotions manifest physically. Stress might settle in your shoulders, while joy might buzz in your fingertips. By identifying these sensations, you become more attuned to your body's signals, allowing you to address them proactively.

Practicing the body scan involves a systematic journey through your body, starting from the tips of your toes and working your way up to the crown of your head. Begin by finding a comfortable position, either lying down or sitting, where you won't be disturbed. Close your eyes and take a few deep breaths to center yourself. Focus your attention on your toes, noticing any sensations, whether they are warmth, coolness, or tension. Slowly move your attention upward, part by part, to your ankles, calves, knees, and so on, acknowledging each sensation without judgment. If your mind starts to wander, gently guide it back to the area you're focusing on. This practice is not about emptying your mind but about fostering a curious, non-judgmental awareness of your body's experiences.

The benefits of body scanning extend beyond mere relaxation. It heightens your self-awareness by enhancing your real-time ability to identify

71

stress and tension. By recognizing these sensations, you can address them before they escalate into major issues. This awareness also promotes emotional clarity and balance as you learn to connect your physical sensations to your emotions. For instance, you might notice a tightness in your chest during stressful situations, signaling anxiety. Acknowledging this connection can empower you to take steps toward emotional regulation, such as practicing deep breathing or engaging in calming activities.

Consider incorporating the body scan into your routine before stressful events, like a big presentation or an important test. This practice can help you ground yourself, reducing the physiological effects of stress and preparing you to perform at your best. Additionally, using the body scan as a nightly routine can help you unwind before sleep, promoting relaxation and restful slumber. As you lie in bed, take a few minutes to scan your body, releasing the day's accumulated tension. This ritual improves sleep quality and instills a sense of peace and inner calm, setting the stage for a rejuvenating night's rest.

Body Scan Checklist

- **Find a Quiet Space**: Choose a comfortable position where you won't be disturbed.

- **Focus on Your Breath**: Take a few deep breaths to center yourself.

- **Scan Your Body**: Start from your toes and move upward, noting sensations in each area.

- **Acknowledge Without Judgment**: Observe sensations without trying to change them.

- **Return Focus When Needed**: Gently guide your mind back if it starts to wander.

By integrating the body scan into your mindfulness practice, you create a deeper understanding of your physical and emotional state. This awareness becomes a powerful tool for self-care, allowing you to deal with life's challenges with greater ease and balance.

8.2 Gratitude Journaling: Focusing on the Positive

Imagine starting your day by jotting down a few things you're grateful for. It may seem simple, but this practice can dramatically shift your perspective. Gratitude journaling is a powerful tool that prompts you to recognize the abundance in everyday life, shifting your focus from what you lack to what you already have. It's about opening your eyes to small yet important blessings, like a friend's laughter, a warm meal, or the comfort of your home. Regularly acknowledging these positives creates a mindset that appreciates the present, enhancing your happiness and contentment.

To make the most of gratitude journaling, it helps to maintain a consistent practice. Begin by writing three things you're grateful for each day. They don't have to be grand; the simplest joys are often the most profound. Think about why these things matter to you as you write, delving into the feelings they evoke. This reflection deepens your gratitude, transforming it from a fleeting thought to a meaningful acknowledgment. Consider using prompts to guide your journaling. Questions like "What made me smile today?" or "Who am I thankful for?" can inspire thoughtful entries. The key is to make this practice a part of your routine, allowing gratitude to weave through your daily life.

Practicing gratitude has real and noticeable benefits for your well-being. By focusing on what you're thankful for, you naturally increase your resilience and reduce stress. Gratitude shifts your mindset, helping you see challenges as opportunities rather than obstacles. This shift boosts your emotional strength, enabling you to handle adversity gracefully. Furthermore, gratitude enhances relationships through appreciation. Recognizing and expressing gratitude for others strengthens bonds and fosters a sense of connection and belonging. These positive interactions enrich your social life, creating a supportive network that uplifts you in times of need.

One gratitude exercise that works is writing letters to friends or family. Take a moment to express why you're grateful for them, focusing on specific qualities or actions that have touched you. These letters are powerful expressions of appreciation and strengthen the relationships you hold dear. Another engaging activity is to host weekly gratitude reflections. Gather with friends or family to share what you're thankful for, encouraging a collective celebration of the positives in your lives. This shared gratitude fosters deeper connections and creates an environment of positivity and support.

Gratitude Journaling Prompt

- **Think about today's highlights**: Write down three things that brought you joy or comfort. Consider what these moments mean to you and why they matter.

Gratitude journaling is more than just a habit; it's a way to nurture a positive outlook on life. By focusing on what you have rather than what you lack, you create a mindset that sees abundance in every day. It transforms ordinary moments into cherished memories, encouraging a deep appreciation for the world around you. As you continue this practice, you'll find that gratitude becomes a guiding force in your life, enhancing your emotional well-being and enriching your relationships with others.

8.3 The Art of Noticing: Finding Joy in Everyday Moments

Imagine walking through your neighborhood, earbuds in, music playing, and your mind on autopilot. It's easy to miss the world around you, the small wonders that fill each corner. Noticing—genuinely paying attention—can transform this mundane walk into a rich experience of sights, sounds, and sensations. This practice of noticing is about cultivating awareness, allowing the present moment to take center stage. It's about finding beauty in the ordinary and joy in the overlooked. When you shift your focus to the details, life unfolds in unexpected, delightful ways, inviting you to engage with the world more deeply.

To practice noticing, start with small, deliberate changes to your daily routine. As you walk to school or work, shift your gaze from your phone to the trees lining the street. Observe the way their leaves flutter in the breeze, the patterns of light and shadow they create. This simple act of observing nature can ground you, pulling you out of your thoughts and into the moment. Similarly, mindful eating can transform a routine meal into an experience. Focus on the flavors, textures, and aromas of each bite. Notice the crunch of a fresh apple or the sweetness of a ripe strawberry. By giving your full attention to these sensations, you deepen your appreciation for the nourishment they provide.

The benefits of noticing extend beyond quickly passing moments of pleasure. This practice enhances mindfulness, increasing your presence in daily life. By cultivating this awareness, you foster a deeper connection with yourself and your surroundings, promoting emotional balance and contentment. This heightened mindfulness helps you respond to life's challenges with equanimity, as you're more attuned to your emotions and can manage them with clarity. The act of noticing also builds gratitude as you become more aware of the richness and abundance in your life. This gratitude strengthens your emotional well-being, creating a positive feedback loop that supports overall happiness.

There are practical ways to incorporate noticing into your routine. Start with a simple noticing challenge: commit to identifying five new things each day. These can be as small as the intricate pattern on a leaf or the way sunlight dances on a puddle. This practice trains your mind to seek out novelty and beauty, keeping your perspective fresh and engaged. Another engaging activity is mindful photography. Take a camera or smartphone and capture images of everyday beauty—an interesting shadow, a vibrant flower, a playful interaction between people. This exercise encourages you to look at your environment with an artist's eye, finding inspiration in the mundane.

Noticing Challenge

- **Daily Goal**: Identify and appreciate five new things each day, whether it's a unique sight, sound, or smell.

- **Document Your Discoveries**: Write them down or take photos to capture these moments.

Practicing the art of noticing enriches your experience of life. It invites you to slow down and engage fully with the world around you. By focusing on the details, you create a sense of wonder and appreciation, transforming ordinary moments into extraordinary ones. This practice can deepen your connection to the present, offering a refuge from the constant pull of distractions. As you refine your ability to notice, you may find that joy is not a distant destination but a thread woven through the fabric of everyday life.

Visualization Techniques: Imagining Your Best Self

Imagine standing at the edge of a tranquil lake, the water reflecting the sky's different hues. As you close your eyes, you picture the life you aspire to live—the goals you wish to achieve, the person you aim to become. This is the essence of visualization, a powerful mindfulness tool that can enhance your focus, motivation, and self-awareness. By using imagery to envision your goals and aspirations, visualization allows you to create a mental picture of desired outcomes. It transforms abstract dreams into vivid realities, providing a roadmap to success.

To practice effective visualization, begin with guided visualizations focusing on personal growth. Find a quiet space where you can relax without interruptions. Close your eyes and take a few deep breaths to center yourself. Imagine a specific goal or aspiration, such as acing your next exam or mastering a musical instrument. Picture every detail of this success—the sights, sounds, and emotions associated with achieving it. Let these sensations fill your mind, creating a vivid mental image that feels tangible and real. Visualization is about seeing and feeling the experience as if it's unfolding in the present moment.

Creating vision boards is another technique that complements visualization. Gather images, words, and symbols that represent your goals and aspirations. Arrange them on a board where you can see them daily, serving as a constant reminder of what you're working towards. Vision boards act as a visual representation of your dreams, reinforcing your commitment to achieving them. They inspire you to take concrete steps toward your goals, turning motivation into action. Regularly engaging with these boards strengthens the connections in your brain associated with your aspirations, making them more attainable and realistic.

The effects of visualization on well-being is profound. Regular practice improves mental clarity and goal orientation as you focus more on what truly matters. Visualization fosters a positive mindset, increasing your motivation and confidence in achieving aspirations. It bridges the gap between where you are and where you want to be, encouraging you to overcome obstacles with determination and resilience. As you visualize success, you encourage a belief in your abilities, empowering you to take on challenges with a proactive attitude.

Engaging in visualization exercises can be both empowering and calming. One exercise is to imagine a successful outcome for a specific challenge you're facing, such as giving a presentation or competing in a sports event. Visualize every step of the process, from preparation to execution, and see yourself succeeding with ease and confidence. This mental rehearsal enhances performance by reducing anxiety and increasing self-assurance. Another exercise is to visualize a relaxing place to reduce stress. Picture yourself in a serene environment, like a beach or forest, and focus on the soothing sensations it evokes. This practice helps alleviate stress and promotes relaxation, providing a mental escape from life's pressures.

Visualization is more than just daydreaming; it's a strategic tool for achieving your dreams. By imagining your best self, you align your actions with your aspirations, paving the way for personal and emotional growth. As you continue to explore the power of visualization, remember that the mind is a powerful ally in shaping your reality. The images you hold in your mind can become your reality, guiding you toward a future filled with possibility and fulfillment. With visualization, you're not just imagining your best self—you're creating it.

Chapter 9:
Integrating Emotional Intelligence into Daily Life

Imagine waking up to the sound of your alarm, the morning sun gently streaming through the curtains, casting a warm glow on your room. You stretch, feeling the promise of a new day, and pause to think about how you'll approach it emotionally. Just like brushing your teeth or grabbing breakfast, what if nurturing your emotional intelligence became a daily habit? Emotional intelligence, much like physical fitness, thrives on consistent practice. It's about embedding small, intentional habits into your routine that gradually build your emotional strength and awareness. It makes it second nature to work through life's ups and downs with poise and insight.

Daily EQ habits are the cornerstone of growing and strengthening your emotional intelligence over time. Consistency is key—small, regular practices can profoundly benefit your emotional well-being. The magic of these habits lies in their simplicity and the way they seamlessly integrate into your daily life. They don't require hours of your time but instead ask for moments of reflection and intention. By incorporating these practices, you create a foundation that strengthens your emotional resilience and adaptability, equipping you to handle whatever comes your way with grace and understanding. Emotional intelligence can be nurtured through habits promoting self-awareness, empathy, and emotional regulation, allowing you to better understand yourself and those around you.

One of the most helpful ways to build emotional intelligence is through morning reflection on emotional goals. Before you get out of bed, take a few moments to consider what emotional qualities you want to embody that day. Maybe you aim to be more patient, more understanding, or more decisive. Setting these intentions aligns your mindset with your goals, creating a roadmap for your emotional interactions. This practice prepares you for the day ahead and serves as a reminder to check in with yourself, fostering a deeper connection with your emotions. It's about starting your day with purpose, ensuring that your actions and reactions are guided by conscious choice rather than impulsive emotion.

Evening gratitude journaling serves as a powerful bookend to your day. As you wind down in the evening, think about the moments and interactions that brought you joy or taught you something valuable. Write them down, acknowledging the positive aspects of your day, no matter how small. This practice shifts your focus from your challenges to the blessings you encountered, reinforcing a positive outlook. Gratitude journaling enhances your emotional well-being and strengthens your ability to find silver linings in challenging situations. It's a gentle exercise in appreciation that encourages a sense of contentment and fulfillment, setting the stage for restful sleep and a positive mindset for the next day.

The effects of these daily EQ habits extends far beyond the immediacy of the moment. They lead to increased self-awareness, allowing you to recognize and understand your emotional triggers and patterns. This heightened awareness enables you to manage your emotions more effectively, choosing responses that align with your values and goals. You'll notice a shift in your relationships as you practice these habits consistently. Regularly reflecting on emotional goals and expressing gratitude nurtures empathy and understanding, strengthening the connections you share with others. Your interactions become more meaningful, guided by a deeper appreciation for the emotions and experiences of those around you.

Maintaining these daily EQ habits requires a commitment to consistency. One practical tip is to set reminders or alarms on your phone for these activities, ensuring they become as routine as brushing your teeth. Associating these habits with existing routines can also be helpful. Consider reflecting on your emotional goals before breakfast or journaling about gratitude just before bed. By pairing these practices with daily activities, they become ingrained in your lifestyle, requiring less conscious effort over time. The key is to approach these habits with patience and understanding, recognizing that building emotional intelligence is a gradual process that unfolds with dedication and time.

Daily EQ Habit Tracker

- **Morning Reflection**: Set your emotional goals for the day; use a prompt like, "Today, I will focus on being [emotion]."

- **Evening Gratitude Journaling**: Every night, write down three things you are grateful for and why.

- **Reminder Setup**: Schedule reminders on your phone to prompt these habits.

- **Routine Pairing**: Decide which existing routine (like breakfast or bedtime) you can pair these habits with.

By cultivating these daily EQ habits, you embark on a journey of emotional growth that enhances your well-being and enriches your relationships. These small, intentional practices become the threads that weave emotional intelligence into the fabric of your life, empowering you to manage the complexities of adolescence and beyond. As you continue to practice these habits, you'll find that emotional intelligence becomes not just a skill but a way of being, guiding you toward a more balanced and fulfilling life.

9.1 The Emotionally Intelligent Teen: Real-World Stories

Meet Alex, a high school junior known for his ability to turn tension into teamwork. In a bustling school environment, where misunderstandings often lead to conflicts, Alex stands out for his knack for defusing tension with empathy. Last year, during a group project in his history class, tensions ran high as different ideas clashed and communication broke down. Instead of letting the situation spiral, Alex stepped in with an empathetic approach. He recognized the frustration brewing among his peers and suggested a moment of pause. With everyone gathered, he encouraged each person to share their perspective, ensuring everyone felt heard. By fostering an environment where students listened to one another, Alex transformed a potential conflict into a collaborative effort. The project succeeded and left the group with a renewed sense of camaraderie and respect. Alex's story illustrates how emotional intelligence can be a tool for creating harmony, even in challenging situations.

Consider Lily, a sophomore who struggled with anxiety in social settings. She often felt overwhelmed and isolated, unable to connect with her peers. However, Lily found solace in a peer-led EQ workshop at her school. The workshop provided a safe space for students to share their feelings and learn from one another's experiences. Through activities focused on empathy and self-awareness, Lily discovered new ways to engage with her emotions. She learned to identify her anxiety triggers and created strategies to manage them, such as deep breathing and visualization. As her emotional intelligence grew, so did her confidence. Lily began participating more actively in class discussions, joined the drama club, and formed meaningful friendships. Her journey highlights the transformative power of emotional intelligence, showing how self-awareness and empathy can lead to personal growth and stronger social bonds.

In another instance, we have Sam, a senior who played a pivotal role in reshaping the dynamics of his school's debate team. At first, the team was plagued by arguments and a lack of cohesion. Sam, who had been learning about conflict resolution in his psychology class, decided to apply these principles to the team. He introduced active listening and perspective-taking techniques, encouraging team members to understand and respect opposing viewpoints. Sam's efforts led to a noticeable shift; debates became more constructive, and the team grew closer. They began winning more competitions, not just because of their skills but also due to their newfound unity. Sam's leadership and application of EQ principles emphasize how emotional intelligence can enhance teamwork and drive success in competitive environments.

These stories reveal valuable lessons about the importance of perseverance and emotional resilience. They show that emotional intelligence is not just about managing one's own emotions but also about fostering empathy and understanding in others. Through their actions, Alex, Lily, and Sam showed that emotional intelligence is a powerful tool for achieving both personal and academic goals. Their experiences underscore the significance of perseverance, as each faced challenges requiring patience and determination. Whether navigating social anxiety, resolving conflicts, or leading a team, their emotional resilience played a key role in overcoming obstacles.

Reflecting on these stories may encourage you to consider your own emotional intelligence journey. This reflection invites you to identify your strengths and areas for growth, asking questions like: What are my emotional triggers? How do I handle conflict? Do I listen actively to my peers? By exploring these questions, you can set personal goals inspired by the experiences of Alex, Lily, Sam and others. For instance, you might aim to improve communication skills or practice empathy in challenging situations. Setting these goals provides direction and motivation, fostering a proactive approach to building your emotional intelligence.

Engaging with emotionally intelligent peers can further enhance this growth. Schools and communities may offer opportunities for teens to connect through peer-led workshops or discussion groups. These spaces encourage sharing and learning from each other's experiences, creating an environment of mutual support. Group projects focused on emotional intelligence can also help create this connection. For example, organizing a community service project where teens practice empathy and teamwork can reinforce EQ skills while making a positive impact. Through these activities, teens can build their emotional intelligence and build a network of supportive peers who share similar values.

Integrating emotional intelligence into daily life transforms it from a concept into a lived experience. The stories of Alex, Lily, and Sam provide a roadmap for how this integration can occur, illustrating the real-world benefits of emotional intelligence. As you think about your own experiences and engage with others, you build the skills and resilience needed to work through the complexities of adolescence and beyond. Emotional intelligence becomes a lens through which you view the world, enriching your interactions and empowering you to create positive change in your community.

9.2 Embracing EQ: From Skill to Lifestyle

Imagine emotional intelligence not just as a skill to be learned but as a way of life, permeating every interaction and decision you make. This perspective transforms EQ from a set of practices into a core value that guides how you move through the world. When embraced as a lifestyle, emotional intelligence offers a holistic approach to well-being. It's about viewing EQ not as a final destination to reach but as an ongoing process that continuously enriches your life. By adopting this mindset, you open yourself to the vast benefits that come from living with emotional awareness and empathy at the forefront of your actions. This lifestyle choice affects everything, from how you handle personal relationships to how you tackle challenges at school or work.

Living an EQ centered life involves practicing mindfulness in all your interactions. Mindfulness in this case is about paying attention to the present moment without judgment. It means listening actively when others speak, acknowledging your emotions as they arise, and responding with intention rather than reacting out of habit. This approach fosters deeper connections with others and a greater understanding of oneself. By being mindful, you create space for empathy and compassion, both toward yourself and those around you. This strengthens your relationships and builds a foundation of mutual respect and understanding. As you engage with others, whether it's a conversation with a friend or a group project at school, your mindful presence can transform ordinary interactions into meaningful exchanges.

Continuously seeking opportunities for emotional growth and learning is another key aspect of integrating EQ into your lifestyle. This means being open to feedback and embracing new experiences that challenge your emotional understanding. It involves stepping out of your comfort zone to engage with diverse perspectives and learning from those interactions. By actively pursuing emotional growth, you enhance your ability to adapt to changing circumstances and work through life's complexities with resilience. This continual learning process enriches your life, allowing you to thrive both personally and professionally. Whether it's reading books on emotional intelligence, attending workshops, or simply reflecting on your experiences, each step toward growth adds depth to your emotional capabilities.

The long-term benefits of adopting an EQ lifestyle are profound. It leads to enhanced personal and professional relationships, as empathy and understanding become the norm in your interactions. These qualities foster environments of trust and collaboration, which are essential for success in any setting. Moreover, an EQ focused lifestyle equips you with greater adaptability and resilience. When faced with challenges, you draw on your emotional intelligence to find solutions, turning obstacles into opportunities for growth. This resilience benefits you and inspires those around you, creating a ripple effect of positivity and progress. As you work through life's ups and downs, your EQ skills serve as an inner compass, guiding you toward fulfillment and balance.

Consider the story of Marcus, a teen who moved to a new city just before his senior year of high school. Initially overwhelmed by the transition, he leaned into his EQ skills to work through this major change. Marcus practiced mindfulness to manage his anxiety, focusing on the present rather than worrying about the unknown. He engaged with his new classmates with openness and curiosity, valuing their perspectives and learning from their experiences. He forged meaningful connections through empathy, transforming his apprehension into a sense of belonging. Marcus's story illustrates how an EQ centered approach can turn daunting transitions into enriching experiences, highlighting the power of emotional intelligence in adapting to change.

In another example, consider community leader Jasmine, who applies her EQ to foster positive change in her neighborhood. Recognizing the diverse backgrounds of her community members, she promotes inclusion and understanding through initiatives that encourage dialogue and collaboration. Jasmine's emotional intelligence allows her to navigate conflicts with grace, finding common ground where others see division. Her leadership style inspires others to embrace empathy, creating a more cohesive and supportive community. Jasmine's work shows how living with EQ as a core value can drive meaningful change, benefiting not just the individual but the collective as well.

These stories show that embracing emotional intelligence as a lifestyle is about more than individual success. It's about contributing to the greater good, using your emotional awareness to make a positive change in your community and beyond. As you incorporate EQ into your daily life, you become part of a larger movement toward empathy and understanding, creating a world where emotions are valued and celebrated. This journey is ongoing, with each step bringing new insights and opportunities for growth. By choosing to live with emotional intelligence, you enrich your own life and positively influence those around you, embodying the quiet strength of your EQ.

Emotional intelligence can be woven into the fabric of everyday life, offering a pathway to deeper connections and personal growth. As you move forward, consider how you can integrate these insights into your daily routine, making EQ a guiding principle in all you do.

Chapter 10: Parental Guidance and Support

Hey parents — this chapter's just for you. Teens, you're totally welcome to read along if you're curious, but heads up: it's more of a grown-up vibe and less of the fun stuff. (Still, might be interesting to see what I'm telling them.)

Imagine a family dinner where everyone gathers around the table, each person with a story to tell, yet the air is thick with unspoken words. This silence, though comfortable, holds back the potential for deeper connections. It's in these everyday moments that the bridge of communication must be built, creating a pathway where thoughts and feelings can flow freely. Open communication between parents and teens is not just nice to have; it's the foundation of trust and understanding. When parents listen without judgment, they offer their teens a safe space to express themselves, fostering a sense of security and belonging. This active listening involves more than hearing words; it requires engagement and empathy, acknowledging emotions without rushing to conclusions.

Opening the channels of dialogue can feel daunting, but it's essential. Start by using open-ended questions, encouraging your teen to share more than just a "yes" or "no." Ask about their day in ways that invite elaborate responses, like "What was the best part of your day?" or "How did you feel during your soccer game?" These questions show genuine interest and pave the way for meaningful conversation. Timing and setting also play crucial roles in initiating these discussions. Choose a moment when you and your teen are relaxed, maybe during a walk or a quiet evening at home, where distractions are minimal, and the focus can be on connecting.

Communication barriers often arise from generational gaps, where parents and teens speak different languages born of distinct experiences and perspectives. To bridge this gap, parents need to recognize and value their teen's unique viewpoints, even when they differ from their own. Embracing these differences as opportunities for learning rather than conflict can transform disagreements into rich exchanges of ideas. Moreover, managing emotional reactions to sensitive topics is vital. When a conversation touches on a delicate issue, keeping emotions in check allows for a more productive dialogue, free from defensive responses.

Practical communication exercises can enhance these interactions, making them more engaging and effective. Regular family meetings to discuss the highs and lows of the week can become a tradition that nurtures openness and transparency. These gatherings provide a platform for everyone to voice their thoughts and feelings, fostering a culture of mutual respect. Joint storytelling sessions can also be a fun way to encourage creativity and sharing. By creating stories together, parents and teens can explore different perspectives, laugh, and connect on a deeper level.

Conversation Starters and Reflective Questions

- What was a moment today that made you smile?

- How do you feel about the challenges you're facing at school?

- If you could change one thing about our communication, what would it be?

These practices help break down communication barriers and build a robust framework for ongoing dialogue. By prioritizing open communication, you create an environment where your teen feels valued and understood, laying the foundation for a relationship that thrives on trust and mutual respect.

10.1 Emotional Coaching: Guiding Your Teen with Empathy

Consider the teenage years as an emotional rollercoaster, where highs and lows come unexpectedly. As a parent, guiding your teen through this ride requires more than just advice; it calls for emotional coaching. This approach centers on empathy, helping teens understand and manage their emotions rather than simply reacting to them. It's about recognizing the subtle cues and signals that indicate how your teen feels, whether it's how they slam their bedroom door after a hard day or the quiet withdrawal at the dinner table. These signs are invitations to engage, not with judgment, but with curiosity and care. Offering empathetic responses means acknowledging their emotions and showing them that you see and hear what they're going through.

Empathetic guidance is a powerful tool in your parenting repertoire. It begins with validating your teen's feelings and accepting them as real and important, even if they seem trivial to you. For instance, if your teen is upset about a lost opportunity, resist the urge to minimize their experience. Instead, acknowledge their disappointment, saying, "I can see how much this meant to you." This validation opens doors to deeper conversations where you can teach problem-solving skills. Guide them through discussing potential solutions, helping them see the situation from different angles. This process empowers them to manage their emotions and equips them with critical thinking skills.

The benefits of emotional coaching extend far beyond the immediate moment. When teens feel understood and supported emotionally, they build trust and security in their relationship with you. This foundation encourages them to come to you with their troubles, knowing they'll find understanding rather than criticism. Moreover, as they learn to work through their emotions, they gain independence and self-confidence, essential traits for adulthood. They begin to trust their ability to handle challenges, turning to you not out of helplessness but for guidance and support.

Emotional coaching is not just a theory but a practice yielding tangible results. Consider the scenario of a teen dealing with the disappointment of not making a sports team. Instead of dismissing their feelings, an emotionally coaching parent might say, "I understand how hard you worked for this. What do you think you could try differently next time?" This approach validates their effort and inspires reflection and growth. Similarly, focus on empathy when guiding a teen through peer relationship complexities. Avoid jumping to conclusions if your teen comes home upset after a disagreement with friends. Instead, ask, "What do you think your friend was feeling?" This question encourages empathy, helping them see the situation from another perspective, often leading to more thoughtful resolutions.

This parenting method fosters an environment where emotions are not feared or ignored but are seen as opportunities for learning and connection. Through emotional coaching, you become a guide, helping your teen manage the intricate landscape of their feelings with confidence and resilience. This approach strengthens your bond with them and prepares them to face life's challenges with empathy and understanding, skills that will serve them well into adulthood.

10.2 Setting Boundaries: Balancing Freedom and Responsibility

Imagine a teenager trying to navigate the vast ocean of adolescence without a compass. This is what life can feel like without clear boundaries. In any healthy relationship, boundaries are the invisible lines defining where one person ends and another begins, promoting mutual respect and trust. They are essential for both parents and teens, providing a framework within which freedom and responsibility can coexist. Consistency in enforcing these boundaries is crucial. When parents maintain clear and steady limits, teens understand what behavior is expected, creating a stable environment where they can explore their independence safely. It's about finding that sweet spot where autonomy flourishes under the umbrella of parental guidance.

Setting effective boundaries requires a collaborative approach. Involving teens in the boundary-setting process empowers them and increases the likelihood of adherence. When teens feel their voices are heard, they are more likely to respect and uphold the agreements made. Start by having open discussions about what boundaries should be in place and why they matter. Clearly communicate expectations and consequences, ensuring everyone understands the rules and what happens if they are broken. This transparency fosters a sense of fairness and mutual understanding, reducing the potential for conflicts down the line.

Of course, setting boundaries is not without its challenges. Teens naturally push back against limitations, testing the waters as they seek to assert their independence. It's a normal part of growing up. However, navigating this resistance requires patience and flexibility. As teens grow and develop, so too should the boundaries. What worked when they were younger will need to evolve to accommodate their increasing maturity and responsibility. This adaptability shows teens that boundaries are not rigid constraints but guidelines that grow with them, accommodating their development into adulthood.

Consider the example of digital device usage. With technology being such an integral part of modern life, establishing rules around screen time is crucial. By setting clear limits on when and how devices can be used, parents help teens balance their online and offline lives. Similarly, negotiating curfews and social outings is another area where boundaries can enhance family dynamics. Allowing teens to have a say in these discussions teaches them about compromise and responsibility. These skills are valuable both now and in the future. When set thoughtfully and enforced consistently, these boundaries guide teens and strengthen family bonds, creating a harmonious home environment.

Case Study: The Digital Balance Act

- Meet Emily, a 15-year-old with a passion for social media. Her parents noticed her grades slipping and decided it was time to set boundaries. They involved Emily in the process, discussing why balance was necessary and agreeing on specific screen time limits. Emily felt respected and was more willing to comply. Over time, her grades improved, and she discovered new hobbies. This shared decision-making process improved Emily's academic performance and strengthened her relationship with her parents, demonstrating the power of well-implemented boundaries.

Boundaries are not about control; they are about fostering a sense of security and trust. They provide the structure within which teens can learn, grow, and thrive, knowing they have the freedom to explore while also feeling the safety net of parental guidance. As these boundaries shift and change with time, they reflect the evolving nature of the parent-teen relationship, adapting to support the unique journey that each family embarks on together.

10.3 Shared Activities: Building Emotional Connections

Think of a bustling kitchen filled with the aroma of spices and laughter echoing off the walls. This vibrant scene is more than just a meal in the making; it's a powerful bonding experience that creates lasting memories. Engaging in shared activities like cooking together can strengthen the emotional fabric of a family. These moments offer a canvas for creativity, where each family member contributes, whether by chopping vegetables or sharing a beloved recipe. As you stir a pot or knead dough, you're not just making food; you're weaving a tapestry of connection and understanding.

Shared activities encourage open dialogue by providing a natural setting for conversation. When hands are busy, mouths tend to open easily, allowing for stories to unfold and interests to be shared. Whether you're discussing the origins of a dish or reminiscing about past vacations, these interactions foster an environment where communication flows effortlessly. Imagine the laughter and storytelling that accompany preparing a family recipe passed down through generations, each anecdote adding flavor to the meal and depth to family ties. Such activities transform everyday routines into opportunities for connection, grounding relationships in shared joy and tradition.

The impact of shared activities extends beyond the immediate joy they bring. They play a crucial role in improving family dynamics, fostering a deeper understanding and empathy among members. When you work together on a community service project, for instance, you contribute to a greater cause and learn about each other's values and dreams. These experiences reduce stress by shifting focus from individual worries to collective goals, enhancing family cohesion. In a world where schedules often pull families in different directions, these shared moments become anchors, reminding everyone of their united strength and purpose.

Consider a family hiking trip as an example of how shared activities can foster teamwork and cooperation. Navigating a trail requires collective effort and decision-making, whether determining the right path or taking turns leading the way. It's a chance to cheer each other on, offering support when the trail gets steep and celebrating together at the summit. These shared triumphs build resilience and trust, showing that challenges become surmountable when faced together. Similarly, a family game night can encourage laughter and bonding, teaching valuable lessons in sportsmanship and strategy. As you roll the dice or make a clever move, you're not just playing a game; you're creating a space where everyone feels valued and connected.

Family Activity Checklist

- Plan a Cooking Night: Choose a new recipe each week, assign roles, and share stories as you cook.

- Organize a Monthly Game Night: Rotate who picks the game to ensure everyone's interests are included.

- Schedule a Hiking Adventure: Explore local trails together, setting goals for each outing to foster teamwork.

- Volunteer as a Family: Find a local charity or community project that resonates with everyone, making service a shared value.

These activities enhance emotional connections and provide a foundation for resilient family bonds. They remind us that the most meaningful experiences often occur not in isolation but in the spaces where we come together, learn from one another, and grow. As these shared activities become traditions, they weave a rich tapestry of memories that fortify family ties, making them stronger and more vibrant with each passing moment.

10.4 The Parent-Teen Contract: Collaborative Goal Setting

Imagine a teenager stepping into the world with a map that outlines their responsibilities and dreams. A parent-teen contract acts like this map, providing clarity and direction by fostering a sense of accountability and mutual respect. At its core, this contract is not a rigid set of rules but a collaborative tool that helps parents and teens clearly outline responsibilities and expectations. It's about creating a shared vision where both parties are committed to achieving common goals, whether they relate to academics, chores, or personal growth. Setting these goals together ensures everyone is on the same page, reducing misunderstandings and building a strong foundation for cooperation.

Creating a parent-teen contract requires thoughtful preparation and open dialogue. Start by involving your teen in the drafting process, ensuring their voice is heard and valued. This participation is crucial for buy-in, as it empowers them to take ownership of their commitments. During discussions, focus on setting realistic and achievable goals. For example, if the goal is to improve grades, outline specific actions like setting aside time for study each night or seeking help from a tutor. These goals should be challenging yet attainable, providing motivation without overwhelming your teen. By collaborating on the contract, you foster a sense of partnership, making the agreement a joint effort rather than a top-down directive.

The benefits of a parent-teen contract extend beyond the document itself. It serves as a living agreement that encourages open discussions about progress and challenges. Regular check-ins to review the contract can become opportunities for constructive conversations, where you and your teen can celebrate achievements or reassess goals as needed. This ongoing dialogue builds a sense of teamwork, reinforcing the idea that you're working together toward shared objectives. It also allows for flexibility, as goals and circumstances may change over time, requiring adjustments to the contract. Maintaining open communication creates an environment where both successes and setbacks are addressed with understanding and support.

Consider a scenario where a contract outlines academic responsibilities and leisure time. For instance, you and your teen might agree that homework should be completed before screen time. This clear expectation helps your teen manage their time effectively, balancing work and relaxation. Another example could be outlining household chores and privileges. You teach your teen the value of responsibility and effort by specifying chores and tying them to rewards or privileges. These agreements contribute to smoother daily routines and instill important life skills, preparing your teen for the independence of adulthood.

Contract Creation Worksheet

- List Areas to Cover: Discuss academics, chores, screen time, and personal goals.

- Define Specific Goals: Set clear, measurable objectives for each area.

- Schedule Regular Check-ins: Plan times to review and adjust the contract as needed.

This chapter has explored various ways parents and teens can strengthen their bond. By embracing open communication, empathetic guidance, clear boundaries, shared activities, and collaborative goal setting, families can grow together. These tools provide a foundation for mutual respect and understanding, helping families navigate the challenges of adolescence with confidence and compassion. As we move forward, we'll delve into integrating emotional intelligence into daily life, exploring how these skills enhance personal development and relationships.

Conclusion

Imagine standing at the edge of a vast ocean, its waves lapping at your feet. Each wave represents an emotion, a thought, or a challenge you've faced on your journey through this book. As you look out at the horizon, you see the endless possibilities that await you, armed with the power of your emotional intelligence.

Throughout our journey together, we've explored the transformative potential of emotional intelligence. We've discovered that EQ isn't just a skill to be learned—it's a strength to be lived. It's the key to unlocking a world of self-awareness, empathy, and resilience. By building your emotional intelligence, you equip yourself with the tools to work through life's ups and downs with grace and understanding.

We've delved into the core concepts of EQ, from recognizing and managing your own emotions to understanding and empathizing with others. You've learned practical strategies for regulating your emotions, communicating effectively, and building resilience in the face of challenges. These skills are not just theoretical; they are applicable to every aspect of your life, from navigating social media and managing academic stress to resolving conflicts and strengthening family bonds.

But the journey doesn't end here. Emotional intelligence is a lifelong pursuit, a daily practice that requires commitment and dedication. I encourage you to integrate the habits and techniques we've discussed into your daily routine. Take a moment each morning to set your emotional intentions for the day. Practice mindfulness in your interactions, listening actively and responding with empathy. Keep a gratitude journal, reflecting on the positive moments and lessons learned. These small, consistent actions will compound over time, strengthening your EQ muscles and transforming how you engage with the world.

As you continue on this path, celebrate the progress you've made. Recognize the courage it takes to look inward, to confront your emotions, and to choose growth. You've taken the first steps in developing your emotional intelligence—and that's something to be proud of. Share your experiences with your peers, inspire them with your example, and foster a community that values emotional intelligence. Together, you have the power to create a ripple effect of positive change, one interaction at a time.

To the parents reading this, your role in your teen's emotional development is invaluable. Continue to practice empathy, listen with an open heart, and create spaces for honest communication. Try shared activities that strengthen your bond and provide opportunities for emotional growth. Encourage the educators at your local school to incorporate EQ in their teaching, or after school opportunities. Your support and guidance are the foundation upon which your teen's EQ will flourish.

Remember, the journey of emotional intelligence is never truly finished. There is always more to learn and more room for growth. Seek resources that deepen your understanding, whether books, workshops, or online courses. Embrace the challenges that come your way as opportunities to flex your EQ muscles and discover new strengths within yourself.

As we conclude this book, I leave you with an empowering message: your emotions are not your weakness; they are your greatest strength. By embracing your emotional intelligence, you unlock a world of possibility. You become the architect of your own happiness, the navigator of your own destiny. With EQ as your compass, you have the power to create a life filled with meaningful connections, personal growth, and boundless potential.

So, as you stand at the shore of your future, know you are ready. You have the tools, the knowledge, and the strength to face whatever waves may come. Step forward with confidence, empathy, and unwavering belief in your own emotional resilience. Life's ocean is vast and unpredictable, but your emotional insight equips you to navigate its depths with courage and curiosity.

Thank you for embarking on this journey with me. Your commitment to personal growth and emotional development is a testament to your strength and courage. As you continue to manage the complexities of adolescence and beyond, remember that your emotional intelligence is your greatest ally. Embrace it, nurture it, and watch as it transforms your world in ways you never thought possible.

References

5 Self-Awareness Activities for Adolescents
https://www.spokaneimagine.com/mental-health-blog/5-self-awareness-activities-for-adolescents/

Here's How Journaling Can Benefit Teens
https://paradigmtreatment.com/journaling-benefit-teens/

Mind-body therapies for resilience in adolescents
https://www.sciencedirect.com/science/article/abs/pii/S016383432400183X

The neurobiology of the emotional adolescent
https://pmc.ncbi.nlm.nih.gov/articles/PMC5074886/

Relaxation Exercises: Breathing Basics (for Teens)
https://kidshealth.org/en/teens/relax-breathing.html

Mindfulness for Teens: Benefits and Practice Tips
https://psychcentral.com/health/the-benefits-of-mindfulness-meditation-for-teens

CBT for Teens: Helping to Reframe Negative Thoughts
https://teenbraintrust.com/cognitive-reframing-a-great-tool-for-parents-teens/

The power of forgiveness https://www.health.harvard.edu/mind-and-mood/the-power-of-forgiveness

40 Empathy Activities & Worksheets for Students & Adults
https://positivepsychology.com/kindness-activities-empathy-worksheets/

How Empathy Maps Can Help Teachers Connect With ...
https://www.edutopia.org/article/how-simple-visual-tool-can-help-teachers-connect-students/

Active listening with pre-teens and teenagers
https://raisingchildren.net.au/pre-teens/communicating-relationships/communicating/active-listening

9 Ways to Embrace Altruism (and Why It Matters) - Personal Growth - eNotAlone https://www.enotalone.com/article/personal-growth/9-ways-to-embrace-altruism-and-why-it-matters-r14063/

Why Teaching Kindness in Schools Is Essential to Reduce ...
https://www.edutopia.org/blog/teaching-kindness-essential-reduce-bullying-lisa-currie

How Using Social Media Affects Teenagers
https://childmind.org/article/how-using-social-media-affects-teenagers/

Cyber-kindness: Spreading kindness in cyberspace
https://mprcenter.org/review/cyber-kindness-spreading-kindness-in-cyberspace/

Digital Boundaries For Generation Z - Understanding Teenagers
https://understandingteenagers.com.au/digital-boundaries-for-generation-z/

Digital Detox for Teens - Eva Carlston Academy Blog
https://evacarlston.com/the-importance-of-digital-detox-how-screen-time-affects-mood-and-mental-health/

3 ways you can help your teen express emotions - Unicef
https://www.unicef.org/parenting/mental-health/3-ways-help-
teens-express-
emotions#:~:text=There%20are%20many%20healthy%20ways
,that%20expresses%20how%20they%20feel.

Youth Conflict Resolution Techniques + Life Skills
https://elcentronc.org/advocacy/youth-conflict-resolution-
techniques-life-skills-processing-conflict-during-a-crisis/

Why the Vocabulary of Emotions is Critical to ... - Presence
https://presence.com/insights/why-the-vocabulary-of-
emotions-is-critical-to-emotional-intelligence/

Unlocking the Power of Nonverbal Communication Skills in ...
https://everydayspeech.com/blog-posts/general/unlocking-
the-power-of-nonverbal-communication-skills-in-elementary-
students-a-social-emotional-learning-perspective/

How to Build Resilience in Children and Teens
https://biglifejournal.com/blogs/blog/how-to-build-resilience-
children-
teens?srsltid=AfmBOoodT_1xW9yVfehf2dK2f8fYAt925EKQ
XsVAnyqlGtPPjt4tBgCV

Famous Failures: 23 Stories to Inspire You to Succeed
https://www.bradaronson.com/famous-failures/

The Growth Mindset Workbook for Teens
https://www.socialworkerstoolbox.com/the-growth-mindset-
workbook-for-teens/

5 Ways Journaling Can Build Your Resilience - Michelle Pearce
https://drmichellepearce.medium.com/5-ways-journaling-can-
build-your-resilience-5b80a3ba7966

Top 10 Stress Management Techniques for Students
https://www.verywellmind.com/top-school-stress-relievers-
for-students-3145179

A parent's guide to handling friendship drama | HealthyU
https://blog.erlanger.org/2020/01/27/friendship-
drama/#:~:text=Let%20your%20child%2Fteen%20fix%20the
%20problem.
:text=But%20most%20normal%20friendship%20drama,solve
%20it%20him%20or%20herself.

9 Family Therapy Activities to Improve Communication
https://overcomewithus.com/parenting/9-family-therapy-
activities-to-improve-communication

How to Teach Children to Control Emotions in Sports
https://www.teamsnap.com/blog/general-sports/how-to-
teach-children-to-control-their-emotions-in-youth-sports

How to Develop a Morning Routine (Teens) (with Pictures)
https://www.wikihow.com/Develop-a-Morning-Routine-
(Teens)

Body Scan Meditation: Benefits and How to Do It
https://www.healthline.com/health/body-scan-meditation

A Brief Gratitude Writing Intervention Decreased Stress and ...
https://pmc.ncbi.nlm.nih.gov/articles/PMC8867461/#:~:text
=Individuals%20with%20higher%20levels%20of,et%20al.%2C
%202015%3B%20Wood

Visualization And Guided Imagery Techniques For Stress ...
https://www.mentalhealth.com/library/visualization-and-
guided-imagery-for-stress-reduction

11 tips for communicating with your teen
https://www.unicef.org/parenting/child-care/11-tips-
communicating-your-teen

An Introduction to Emotion Coaching
https://www.gottman.com/blog/an-introduction-to-emotion-
coaching/

Setting healthy boundaries with your teenager
https://parents.au.reachout.com/parenting-skills/building-trust/setting-healthy-boundaries-with-your-teenager

Create a Teen Behavior Contract
https://parentandteen.com/discipline-adolescent-responsibility-contract/

10 Emotional Intelligence Habits You Can Start Today
https://www.vmapsych.com/resources/10-emotional-intelligence-habits-you-can-start-today

Emotional Intelligence From a Teenage Perspective ...
https://www.youtube.com/watch?v=MbmLNr89L-A

The Importance of Emotional Intelligence (Incl. Quotes)
https://positivepsychology.com/importance-of-emotional-intelligence/

Mindfulness exercises https://www.mayoclinic.org/healthy-lifestyle/consumer-health/in-depth/mindfulness-exercises/art-20046356

www.ingramcontent.com/pod-product-compliance
Lightning Source LLC
Chambersburg PA
CBHW071205120626
46546CB00006B/2429